• OPENING •
• THE DREAM •
• DOOR •

Using Your Dreams for Spiritual and Psychic Development

BY JANICE WINSOR

printed in the United States of America
10 9 8 7 6 5 4 3 2 1

ISBN 1-886708-04-5
Library of Congress Card Number 98-066082

All artwork in this book by Janice Winsor © 1998

Cover Art by Janice Winsor
Cover Design by Morris Design, Monterey, California
Edited by Ann West, Carmel, California
Interior design by Danielle Shillcock, Monterey, California

MERRILL-WEST PUBLISHING
P.O. Box 1227
Carmel CA 93921
831 • 644-9096
e-mail: info@voyagertarot.com
web site: www.voyagertarot.com

CONTENTS

ACKNOWLEDGMENT

To Fred

because it was all his idea in the first place.

1

THE DREAMS SPEAK

"NEW RAM"

I dream of an old while-haired man with a player piano. He has rooms and rooms of piano rolls that are the recordings of people's life patterns. He plays a concert for me.

The Player Piano
– March 1983

All my life, I've had dreams like this one, even when I was going about the business of living, totally unconscious of any higher purpose in life. I had dreams that showed a glimpse into other dimensions, different ways of thinking about life or dealing with perceptions. My emotional response to these dreams was always one of awe, wonder, and exhilaration. The feelings would stay with me for days, sometimes for weeks. And then I'd go back to living my life and forget about them.

I believe that these dreams were communications from my higher self, from other dimensions, and from the psychic realm. I want to share some of them with you and to suggest that your dreams can also be a door into another dimension. I would like to help you open that dream door and become more sensitive to messages from other dimensions. I have had thousands and thousands of dreams about everyday life, its problems and issues. I have plenty of those kinds of dreams. But when I dream about the other realms, the sensations, emotions, and feelings of recognition are unmistakable. The "special" dreams stand out with a luminosity and clarity uniquely their own. In addition, these high spiritual dreams often feel like recurring dreams, even though I seem to dream them only once. The feeling of familiarity and recognition has become one of the hallmarks of such dreams. I believe that the familiarity is not with the content of the dream itself, but with the truth and connection to those other dimensions. Now, when I say, "I have had this dream before," I recognize that what I really mean is I have been to this dimension before.

I've also had many dreams in which it seemed to me that the ultimate secrets of the universe were revealed. Then I'd wake up and say "Now, what was that ultimate secret?" I could remember that there was a secret, but not what it was.

I'm not the only one who has high spiritual dreams. Because my dreams are so much a part of my life, I often share them with friends and fellow workers. I remember a conversation with a secretary I worked with many years ago. She had a dream that she characterized as "disturbing" and wanted to talk to me about it. She dreamed of an old white-haired man. She said, "He looked like God." Her old white-haired man did not have a room full of piano rolls. Instead, he had a huge book that contained the recordings of people's life patterns. As he turned the pages, she saw what seemed to her to be movies of other people's lives. She did not understand why she was given this information and did not want the responsibility of knowing how to access it. She was afraid of this dream and what it meant.

I believe both my dream and her dream were about the place where all of the information about our incarnations and past lives is stored—the place called the Akashic Records. Her dream of the Akashic Records was like a multimedia presentation; mine was in musical form. I'm sure both dreams were equally valid, either way.

So, why was her dream a disturbing experience and mine an exhilarating one? The secretary had been raised Catholic, as was I. But she had not shifted her belief framework to incorporate the concept of past lives, as I had done. And the reason I believe I was successful in shifting my beliefs was because of all the groundwork that had been laid in my dreams over the years by my higher self, my spirit guides, and my animal allies. Once I started paying more attention to the dreams of other dimensions, I did lots of reading and exploration, took workshops with gifted teachers, and discussed the information avidly with friends.

Many excellent books have been written about why we dream and how to interpret and use dreams to solve day-to-day problems. I do not want to cover the same territory or try to compete with other books. Instead, I begin where most books stop, with information about how I believe you can use your dreams to connect to the spiritual and psychic realms. I share a few of the special dream gifts I've received so you can see specific examples of them. I also suggest how you can open your dream door to these realms.

From my dream journal, I selected some of my favorite dreams to include in this book. They are grouped into chapters on nine different topics:

- **Creativity**—Use dreams to tap in to your creative energies and to solve problems in your day-to-day life.

- **Healing dreams**—Heal your body.

- **Great teachers**—Experience profound truths (like my ultimate secrets dreams) from great teachers.

- **Animal allies**—Become familiar with the animals that are with you by recognizing them and working with them in your dreams.

- **Past lives**—Dream about past life experiences and understand past-life connections with people in your world.

- **Channeling**—Open yourself to channeled information, establishing connections that may carry forward into your waking state.

- **Rites of passage**—Recognize when shifts and changes are occurring in your life.

- **Psychic experiences**—Receive precognitive dreams and connect with people who are no longer here in a physical body.

- **Alien encounters**—Connect with alien energies and realize that you may have experienced life on another planet.

Although categories can be useful in some contexts, be aware that identifying dreams by a specific type can be a bit of a trap. For example, many dreams in this book do not fit neatly into just one category. Some have elements that might fit into several of these categories. So, when you work with your own dreams, be aware not to be too literal or restrictive in assuming that a particular dream fits into only one category. In fact, there may well be other categories that you decide fit your dreams better than the ones I've chosen for this book.

The following two dreams do not seem to fit into the above categories.

> *I dream I speak with a water spirit who lives in the base of a huge ancient oak tree. The tree has a ring of burls around the base of the trunk that reaches as high as my knees. A spring spouts water out of the top of the burls. Someone shows me how to put a strange kind of a keyboard under the water and to play it to communicate with the water spirit.*
>
> *And the water spirit speaks and, in silvery, burbling tones, says things like, "You're running out of laundry soap." In this teaching, I learn to respect attention to detail and the trivial, as well as to the wonder and beauty of it all. I am given permission to communicate with the water spirits at any time.*

Then a wood spirit comes and teaches me how to magically shape deer bones into bracelets and amulets that let me move with the grace and the spirits of the deer.

I learn how to understand the essence of what it is to be a spirit being and, hence, to transmute and transcend the essence of the physical body and to leave behind all fear of death and change.

I become a nymph, a wood sprite, the deer, and all of nature. I can go back there at any time.

Water Spirit
–December 25, 1994

I had this dream on Christmas morning, 1994. The previous night, I dreamed that a wood nymph was going to teach me to move in secret paths by following the scent of the green grass snake. Just at the point when I said, in my dream, "But I don't know what a green grass snake smells like," one of my cats came to the window, woke me up, and wanted me to let her in out of the rain. I tried and tried to continue the dream that my cat had interrupted because I was sure the wood nymph was going to take me to some place very special and wonderful. Later, as I was writing down the dream about the water spirit, I realized with amazement and joy that it described where the wood nymph of the previous night had been trying to take me.

This dream is very magical and empowering in its connection to the energies of Mother Earth and Father Sky. It's also a powerful reminder of how strongly connected we can be with the primal energies of the earth. I found it amusing that I had such a Pantheistic dream on Christmas morning. The Water Spirits dream has nothing and everything to do with the Christ message that we are all one and that the kingdom of heaven is within each of us.

The magic of the Water Spirit dream motivated me to get back to work on this book, which had been lying fallow for 14 months. As I looked through the dreams to include, I rediscovered a dream fragment about a green grass snake that I had back in July 1989 (see the chapter about our animal allies). This vibrant spring green fellow has evidently been slithering through my dreams for some time.

Many people have a fear or aversion to snakes. They may not know snakes symbolize the power of transformation. I do not fear snakes, nor am I repelled by them. I do respect the power and danger of poisonous snakes and give them wide berth. The green grass snake is small, slender, harmless, and sweet.

Rediscovering the green grass snake in my dreams has reminded me once more of the value of keeping a dream journal. I do not record all of my dreams by any means. I always think, "Well, I won't forget that dream." And then, of course, I do. If you don't already keep a dream journal, I suggest you begin. If you want to remember your dreams better, check the bibliography at the back of this book for suggestions of other excellent books on dream work. Because working with the ideas and types of dreams in this book can be quite a commitment, you can be somewhat selective in deciding which dreams to record.

The next dream is a dream of teaching and initiation.

> I am initiated into a knowledge called the "Tears of Mystery." Start with three pink rosebuds. Following written instructions, unfold one of the rosebuds and, petal by petal, gently rub the inner surface of the petal with either a brand new dime or an old penny. Watch the surface to see what appears.

> As I rub the petals, at first I see nothing much. Looking at the instruction sheet, I see a list of tarot cards. Gradually images begin to emerge from subsequent

petals. Then I pick up the pile of petals. Complete pictures of tarot cards emerge, along with the names of the major arcana in a yellow rectangle with black letters.

I am amazed and overwhelmed. I go to find a friend to share in this marvelous experience, but she is busy. I go back into the basement laboratory and am distressed to learn that the cleaning lady has moved the roses. However, I find that the petals have been neatly stacked and put aside. I take them and the two remaining rose-buds and go home to complete my studies alone.

Tears of Mystery
—June 1985

The dream is one of many teaching dreams I have experienced. In this dream I am being introduced to a new method of learning. Although I want to share my discovery, I find that I, alone, must learn the information before I can share it with others. At the time I had this dream, I was just beginning to explore and learn the tarot. Oddly enough, 15 years before, I had read a book that was based on the major arcana of the tarot, and I had been interested enough to go out and buy a Waite-Ryder deck. I took the cards home, looked at them and at the instruction pamphlet, and thought, "The tarot is too complicated and I'll never figure it out." I placed the cards back into their box and put them on a bookshelf. Fifteen years later, after I had my first tarot reading, I went looking for the cards, and I could not find them. They had vanished from my house. So I went out and bought a new and different deck. I was now ready, so the tarot seemed easy and intuitive to learn.

I often find, when I encounter new things, that the learning continues into the dream state. It is as though my mind continues processing and integrating the new information. My dreams "wrap around" the new insights and provide a context and framework for understanding.

I believe that our consciousness is a continuum between the waking and dreaming state. In fact, the more I worked on this book, the more I realized this. When you pay attention to your dream messages, you also pay more attention to those hints and intuitions in your waking state. And, the more aware you are in the waking state, the easier it is to recognize and interpret your dream messages.

So, how can you open your dream door? One excellent way that has worked for me for many years is to prepare my mind and spirit for sleep and dreams anticipating the dream door to open. I meditate in bed as preparation for sleep. If I want an answer to a question, I formulate a simple question and repeat it like a mantra as I am drifting off into sleep. I expect my dreams to answer my questions. And when I wake up, I write down whatever I remember. The very act of writing is like pulling a thread. At first you have only the thread, but as you pull, more and more thread emerges from the hidden source, and soon you have a massive tangle of a story that is your dream.

The answer to your dream questions do not always come in your sleep, however. You may be disappointed you didn't get a dream answer, but sometime that day, or in the next few days, you'll have a breakthrough thought while you're driving. Or a book that answers your question may just accidentally fall off the shelf into your hands.

Recently, I heard a report about sleep research on the radio. The researchers were curious to know what people's sleep patterns would be if they had no artificial light or stimulation during the nighttime hours. They wired up their subjects with electrodes and had them sleep from the time the sun went down until the sun rose again in the morning.

The first few weeks, the subjects slept the entire time the sun was set. After they had made up any sleep debt with this intensive period of sleeping, the subjects slept between 8 and 9 hours a night. The rest of the time, up to 4 hours a night, the subjects' brain waves looked like those belonging to expert meditators.

The subjects reported that while they were doing this study, they felt more rested, alert, and mentally able and capable during the day and that they did not miss reading in bed, watching television, or any of the other activities that they had to give up during the period of the experiment.

Unfortunately, none of the subjects were on the air to share their subjective impressions of the experiment. I would like to have heard the descriptions of how the time passed when they were not actually asleep.

Nevertheless, I feel I can answer this question and provide my own description of this quality of time. Although I do not go to bed with the chickens or get up with the roosters, I have spent many hours in a state that is not sleep, but is more like meditation. In fact, the insomnia that used to plague me from time to time is not an issue any more. I don't worry about whether I'm actually asleep or not. I just hang out in those places between waking and sleeping. In fact, a few years ago, I discovered that this state, for me, is like waking sleep. Let me explain.

When our brains are active, they emit brain waves at a frequency called beta, the fastest of the normal brain waves. When we are in creative waking state, relaxed and alert, we emit slower alpha waves. When we are in a deep trance or meditative state, our brains emit even slower theta waves. And when we sleep, our brains emit the slowest, delta, waves.

A few years ago, I was fortunate enough to take both alpha and theta biofeedback training classes. In these classes, students were wired with electrodes pasted onto their scalps. We were put in individual rooms where sound feedback told us whether we were producing the desired brain waves. The louder the noise of our equipment, the more successful we had been. The immediate audio feedback told us how well we were doing. The instructors provided tips on things to try during these private and personal sessions. At the end of the session, we were shown the tracings of our brain waves, and we discussed subjective experiences.

When I meditate, I see a deep purple light. Sometimes the light is a pulsing purple spot in front of me. Other times, the purple comes in sweeping waves. I was curious to know what my brain waves were doing when I got into this state.

In the alpha feedback training, the minute I got to the place where I saw the purple, the sounds dropped to almost nothing. So I knew that my purple place was not in the alpha brain waves. I went on with the rest of the class and was quite successful in achieving the alpha state.

A few months later, I signed up to take the theta feedback training. The theta state is harder to achieve, and the sessions were much longer to give the students a greater chance to succeed. The instructor suggested that one way to achieve the theta state was to head towards sleep and then level out just before you get there. I was still curious about my purple place, and found out that it was not theta either.

Alpha and theta waves are emitted by different parts of the brain, the electrodes for the theta training were in a different place. When I was in my purple place, the brain waves from the second class showed something that some scientists believe is not possible: waking delta. Because delta waves represent the brain when it is sleeping, it seems a paradox to be awake and asleep at the same time. Yet I do it all the time. I just didn't know I was routinely achieving the impossible.

Although it is rare for me to see visual images when I meditate, I saw images and visions that were very dream-like in both alpha and theta states.

The radio report of the sleep research did not identify the particular brain waves that they considered meditative. They could have been theta, or possibly waking delta. Of course, you do not need to know what particular frequency your brain is emitting when you sleep or when you meditate to do either successfully.

I believe the purpose of meditation is not just to clear out the mind so that it is blank and receives no input. I believe that when we relax enough and clear our mind of its daily clutter and get into a deep meditative state, we connect to the higher realms. Call it your higher self, your spirit guides, god, goddess, all that is. Whatever you call it can give you answers and guidance.

I recently completed a hypnotherapy training class in which I became even more familiar with brain wave patterns and how to use them to help people make profound transitions in their thought patterns. Since I've been helping people with hypnotherapy, the borderline between waking and sleeping states seems to have become even more diffuse. Many people experience the trance state of hypnotherapy work as though it were a dream. I feel even more strongly that consciousness is a continuum and each state of mind affects all others.

I firmly believe that we are all guided. We are none of us alone in this lifetime. We have spirit guides, angels, animal allies, teachers, and on and on who wish us well and are always there to give us a helping hand. All we need to do is ask. These guides and guardians can be in physical bodies, but many are not. Sometimes the guidance can seem very subtle, like a passing thought. Or it can look like a coincidence. For example, having someone offhandedly mention that a class you're interested in taking is now being offered.

Furthermore, I believe answers and guidance come to us during our dream state. They can also come when we're wide awake and not meditating. But most people don't trust their instincts, their own little voices, enough to recognize these hints, answers, and little nudges when they're in a mode of normal consciousness.

One reason to work with your dreams as well as your meditations is to enable yourself to recognize your spirit guides and messengers in a different but related arena—

the dream state. Once the door has opened, you are likely to find that you begin to recognize them when you are awake as well. I realize more and more there is no firm dividing line between the meditative state, the dream state, and the waking state. It's all a continuum. And when you work on getting connected to the spirit realms through your dreams, through your meditations, or through your waking state, the more you will know that these states become interconnected. The distinction becomes relatively unimportant.

For me, opening the dream door and acknowledging the information and messages I was receiving were my ways to walking the path toward enlightenment. It is for this reason I want to share my experiences and insights with you. This book contains my own dreams and the lessons I have learned from them. It is a deeply personal book. I hope you will be able to see how the connections are made from the dream state into conscious awareness and understand how to move forward with your own learning and growth. I also hope you will be able to use your dreams as a key to awakening consciousness.

To open the dream door, try the following procedures:

- Prepare yourself for sleep as though it is not a shutting down of senses but instead an opening up of them.

- Meditate before going to sleep, either before you go to bed or while you are lying in bed preparing to sleep.

- If you have a particular question you would like answered by your dreams, incubate the dream by formulating a simple question and repeating it to yourself as you drift off to sleep.

- Write down your dreams as often as you can, or keep a tape recorder by your bed and record your impressions as soon as you awake. Practice in dream recall, like in anything else, produces results.

- Expect miracles.

2

CREATIVITY

"ULTIMATE SECRETS"

I am in the museum of creativity. Each room has wonderful things in it. The museum contains paintings, sculptures, inventions, thoughts, ideas, new ways of eating, new ways of being. I walk from room to room amazed by the *inventiveness and beauty of the things I see. The museum is immense, and each room leads to another with even more fabulous creations in it. I awake with tears in my eyes because I can only remember the idea of the beauty and not of the individual creations.*

Museum of Creativity

I have visited the Museum of Creativity many times in my dreams. In addition, I've dreamed poems, paintings, sculptures, and words in other languages that I do not know in waking life.

Your dreams can be a way to tap into the creative energy that lies within you. I hear many people say, "Oh, I'm not creative." "I can't paint." "I can't draw." "I can't write." And so on. I used to say these kinds of things myself. And then I began to say, "I can." I took drawing and painting classes and found out I am rather good. I began to do technical writing for a living and found I have a gift for translating technical gibberish into plain English ordinary folks can understand. Not only that, but I have come to understand that creativity comes in all shapes and sizes. It can be as simple as knowing the exact right thing to say to another person to help them over a tough emotional situation or to get them "unstuck" and moving forward with a new idea. It can also be intuitively picking the perfect gift for a person.

I believe each individual is a unique being who has only to open to the possibility of being creative to allow those energies to unblock and to flow.

The dictionary defines *creative* as "resulting from originality of thought, expression, etc." and then refers to imagination. *Imagination* is defined as "forming mental images or concepts of what is not actually present to the senses; a conception or mental creation; ability to meet and resolve difficulties; resourcefulness."

To be able to create, you must first imagine, or form an image in your mind of what you want to bring forth. Creativity and imagination are synergistic concepts that work together to bring forth a whole that is more than the sum of the parts.

And, although many people say, "Oh, I'm not creative," you often hear the same people saying, "Imagine that." If you can imagine something, then you have already begun the creative process. Here's the ultimate creativity dream about the blueprint of life.

> *I am with two other people—a man and a young boy. We are in a place with a high rocky top to it and are trying to figure out how to get to the top. It looks impossible. I have a small-scale model*

of the mountain top and am
holding it in one hand and tracing
a route to the top with a pencil.
Then, as the pencil gets to the
top, I am on top of the mountain
looking down to the level below.
There are all sorts of animals on
top in little pockets of rock—
lizards, bobcats, and others. I yell
down, "Look at all the animals
up here," and the man says,
"Who put them there?" I say,
"No one." He says, "Where are
the cages and leashes." I say,
"No, they're wild and free."

I look down from the top, which is
bare granite, to the next level
where the man is, which is red
sandstone like Ayers Rock in
central Australia. He goes over
to the edge of the sandstone to
peer further down, and I say,
"What's that by your foot?" He
doesn't see and finally notices and
picks up a scale model of a
bullock which is next to a model
of a man. These models (and
others) are in a row looking out

off the edge of the bluff. There
are giant inscriptions incised in
the rock and I realize these are
blueprints or formulas for crea-
tion. They represent the African
branch.

African Blueprint
−August 1982

This dream reconnected me to past life incarnations in both tribal Africa and as an Australian aborigine.

Although I thought I remembered this dream quite vividly, over time my creative mind transmuted it into a vision of an African woman sitting on a cliff over-looking the great rift valley creating scale model animals out of red clay. A storyteller says my creative reinterpretation of this dream matches archetypal creation myths.

So, how can you get in touch with your creative energies? Consider your dreams as a way to unleash this part of you. But, if you do not think your dreams are creative, then likely they will not be. Years ago I saw a psychiatrist for a time who envied the richness and imagery of my dreams. He used to say, "All I dream about are things like going to the grocery store with my children." At the time, I was intent on unraveling the confusion of my life situation. So I didn't make any suggestions to him about how to dream more creatively.

However, to you I suggest that the Museum of Creativity is always open, that the blueprint of creation is available to you as well. You can use your dreams to solve problems or to write poems. I've written poems in my dreams and then written them down upon waking only to find that they were the most appalling doggerel. Nevertheless, Coleridge reputedly wrote "Kubla Khan" because of a dream, and a chemist solved the problem of the molecular structure of benzene through a dream. I recently bought a CD called *Medicine Woman* by a musician named Medwyn Goodall, which I found very compelling. I called to order more of his CD's, and the woman who promotes his work in this country told me Medwyn dreams all of his music.

One reason I believe dreams can help you creatively solve problems is that they can make the right-brain intuitive leap to a solution while bypassing the linear left-brain thinking Western society believes is the vehicle for methodically working through issues.

Linear left-brain thinking certainly has its place, and I am grateful to those such as bankers and accountants who manage such functions for us. But the essence of creativity is to make the intuitive jump that I believe lies firmly in right-brain nonlinear thinking.

For a while, I was a mentor in a company-organized program where fellow employees were asked to assist other employees in the organization. One of the individuals I mentored was asking for help because his manager thought he was too tactical and needed to be more strategic.

Although I have always been quite strategic, I was concerned about whether I could teach this man to do what I naturally and intuitively know how to do. We worked together for several weeks, and one day stumbled onto the root cause of the issue. Tactical is left-brain and strategic is right-brain thinking. We then started working with Betty Edwards' excellent book *Drawing on the Right Side of the Brain*. As I reread the book and started working through some of the exercises with my fellow employee, I came to understand in a conscious way some of the patterns and habits I had used unconsciously up until then. I learned things about myself in this process that I had never expected.

For example, Betty Edwards suggests that driving is a very right-brain activity. It involves spatial relations and pattern recognition. If I have a difficult problem to solve or something to think over, I always get in my car and go for a long drive. After such a drive, I almost always come back with a solution or an answer. For a long time I didn't know why it worked, I just knew that it did. And the reason is that I metaphorically throw all of the elements together into the soup kettle and put the problem on the back burner while I go for a drive. While I'm driving, which activates right-brain functions, the right-brain looks at the problem, or goes into the pot, if you will, and answers the question, "Is it soup yet?"

Here's a simple example of this process that I remember clearly. I was writing a quick-reference guide for system administrators. The concept of the book itself, although obvious to me, was perceived as quite creative within the company. I needed a title for this book that reflected its uniqueness. So, one lunch hour, I drove from Mountain View, California, to Half Moon Bay and back. When I returned, I had the title, *The How-To Book*. Now, this title may not seem very creative, but considering the titles of other documents that went with this book, it was quite radical. And we used it.

Creative solutions to problems come to us not only in our dreams but when we shift our state of consciousness. When you stop worrying about finding a solution, often the answer emerges naturally and intuitively.

As I worked with my fellow employee on the exercises in Betty Edwards' book, it seemed we were not addressing the issue of getting more strategic. At the same time, we also worked on some specific tasks and issues related to work. My co-worker was a willing guinea pig in this experiment, even though it often seemed like we were just playing around and not "working on the problem." However, the right-brain exercises did work amazingly well. After a few months, I got a thank you message from my co-worker's manager and the employee got a better performance evaluation.

From this mentoring experience, not only did I learn many things I had been unaware of about myself and my own mental processes, but I also learned that you can teach creativity!

Granted, these examples all took place in what we call waking reality. Yet, the dream state can be used every bit as effectively to turn on the right side of the brain and give it a problem to solve.

Consider dreams. They are usually highly visual and leap from subject to subject in some of the most amazing ways, pulling together disparate elements in a very innovative and creative manner. Just before Christmas in 1993, I wrote down a fragment from a dream.

> *Dreams can hand you a memory key.*
>
> *Memory Key*
> *– December 22, 1993*

I believe we can use the memory keys that dreams hand us to unlock innovative solutions to questions about relationships, career, personal growth, or anything else however mundane or earth-shattering. Usually we already know the solution to a problem and the answer needs only to be acknowledged.

For example, at one time in my life, I was in a very difficult relationship with a man I was very much in love with. I asked my dreams one night to give me insight into where this relationship was going. And I got a very clear answer. I dreamed about a Porsche that had four flat tires. In waking life, this man did, in fact, own a Porsche, and the car in my dream was just like his car. My dream told me quite clearly this relationship was not going anywhere.

Sometimes, dream answers are a bit more obscure and difficult to interpret, but I believe our higher self keeps sending us messages until we get them.

Of course, sometimes we get answers without consciously having asked a question. Even had I not asked my dreams for an answer, I believe I would have been able to accurately interpret this particular dream image.

I have heard many people say that dreams tell you something you don't already know about yourself. I disagree with this sweeping statement. I believe many times our dreams confirm things we already know intuitively that our rational minds may not allow us to accept as true.

Asking your dream for answers is called incubating a dream. The technique is quite simple. First you formulate your question. The simpler the question, the less ambiguous the answer is likely to be. The more issues you throw into the pot, the harder it may be to decide which part of the dream is the answer to which part of the question. Some examples of short, simple questions are as follows:

- Where is this relationship going?

- Do I really want this job?

• Is this house the right one for me to live in?

After you have formulated your question, write it down so you can remember the exact phrasing. Then before you go to sleep, state your intention to have a dream that answers the question. Repeat the question several times as you prepare yourself for sleep. If you wake up in the middle of the night, write down any dream fragments you remember. If you don't remember any dreams during the night or when you wake up in the morning, you may find that, sometime during the following day, an idea or phrase will seem to just pop into your head. Pay attention to these seemingly random thoughts. Sometimes the mind does not respond in the dreamtime, but does it while you're awake instead. In fact, you may get your answer from another person, or from a chance encounter or seemingly random comment.

Remember that consciousness is a continuum between dreaming and waking states. Don't be so locked in to the concept that you're supposed to get an answer in a dream that you ignore the answer when it comes to you when you're awake. The right brain is working away on the problem you have given it to solve.

When you think you have an answer, how do you know how to interpret it? First, go back and look at the question you wrote down. Sometimes a key word within the question will be the trigger for the dream response. Dreams frequently like to respond with puns. So if you ask yourself where is this relationship going and you dream about a shipwreck or a romantic cruise ship, it's the "ship" part of relationship that your dream self chose to use as the memory key to answer the question.

It's a good idea to pay special attention to dream puns, particularly with names. If, for example, you ask where is this relationship going and you have a dream about Paul Newman, perhaps it's time for a new man in your life. (Sorry, I don't know who the new woman dream pun person might be.)

Discuss the dream with a friend, not so the friend can interpret the dream, but so you can hear how you describe it to someone else. Listening to your own narrative of a dream can sometimes give you answers you didn't recognize when you pondered the dream by yourself.

You can ask other people's opinions about what a dream means, but you are responsible for your own dream imagery. Another person's interpretation of a dream or its images is not a valid interpretation unless you feel an "aha" of recognition when you hear it. If the interpretation doesn't seem right to you, then it's not the right interpretation for your dream. To avoid having the other person tell you what the dream means, it's a good idea for him or her to say, "If it were my dream, x would mean this and such." That way you may be less likely to feel like your dream is being misinterpreted if you don't resonate with the interpretation.

In addition to asking your dreams for answers to questions about issues in your life, I urge you to look to your dreams for creative and innovative new things you can do. As I mentioned before, I have dreamed complete paintings. But, I've also done paintings of dream images that were compelling or even bizarre. Here's one of my "ultimate secrets" dreams that I turned into a painting.

> I am on the second flight of the space shuttle and there is a procedure to be followed before reentry starts. I am chosen to be part of the chain of people holding together some kind of linking device. When it engages we go into free-fall. Then something catastrophic happens. We are floating out in space over a plain of clear lucite. We suddenly realize a fundamental truth: Dead people become teddy bears. We float over a huge storage area filled with them.
>
> Ultimate Secrets #72
> –June 1981

This is a strange ultimate secret, but the imagery stuck with me and I turned it into a painting.

I've also had long and very complicated dreams that could be turned into plots for novels or science fiction tales. So far, I've chosen not to use the creativity of my dreams in this way. But you need not follow my example.

Thirty years ago, I had a dream about a deer that had suction cups on its antlers and they kept getting stuck together. I told the dream to my husband, and he was charmed by it. He thought I should write a children's book based on the dream. Although I haven't done so yet, it may happen some day.

In the recent TV program "The Beatles Anthology," Paul McCartney tells how he woke up one morning with the tune for "Yesterday" in his head. It seemed very familiar to him. He worked it out on the piano and added some chords, and then went around and asked lots of people where the tune was from. In fact, it was a completely new and original tune that had come to him while he was dreaming. But it seemed so familiar and he thought it was "too easy" that he had just dreamed it up! Later in the program he talked several times about some of his most creative ideas appearing to him in that space just between waking and sleeping, "where you see all the strange stuff."

To help you see how just one dream can affect your life creatively, I give you the following example.

> *I am to use my Rite of Passage dream as an example in the Creativity chapter of "Opening the Dream Door."*

Creative Suggestion
—August 4, 1995

The Creative Suggestion dream is a very specific and unencrypted dream that tells me how to proceed further with this chapter in the book. And here is the dream.

I am in a jeep with six people. One of them is a former boyfriend, another a very creative but troubled artist friend. We are on a trek to a mountain site where a rite of passage is to take place.

We drive up and spend the night sleeping in the jeep. I dream all night about weird and wondrous things and am not afraid. In the morning, others in the car complain that they had not slept at all because the dog who had driven the jeep had been sick all night. I know nothing of this, saying I slept soundly and had marvelous dreams. The artist says she, too, slept well. They want to know if I am afraid of these dreams and I say no, just curious.

The artist had already gone through this rite and chosen to stay on a certain level and not complete the initiation. She liked where she was.

The location is very rocky and craggy. They lead me around into a sort of rocky cave, and there is one of the images I had dreamed the night before: a white ram lying on its head upside down against the rocky wall. And I say, fantastic. I believe I dreamed the whole rite already. Is that the point? And they say YES!

Rite of Passage
—April 7, 1982

Now, I must confess, I didn't really understand this dream right away, but I was definitely intrigued by it, by the dream within the dream and the layers and complexity of the rite of passage. The dream stayed with me, but I did not expend much energy trying to understand it.

Some months after I had this dream, I took a dream workshop with Dr. Patricia Garfield, a well-known leader in the field of dreamwork and dream analysis.

One of the things we did in the workshop was to work with a significant dream that we didn't yet understand. I chose to work with the Rite of Passage dream. We were led through a guided visualization in which we were asked to communicate with someone or something in the dream that we wanted to understand more about. I chose to dialog with the upside-down white ram. And when we were instructed to ask the dream messenger for its name, my ram said his name was Creativity.

After the visualization, we broke up into groups to discuss our experiences. I still did not understand completely what the cave and the ram were all about. Working with the group helped me understand that the cave represented the womb and that the ram, in its upside down position against the wall of the cave, was in the birthing position and ready to emerge into the world. So the message of the dream is that I was ready to give birth to creativity.

At this time in my life, I was very stuck creatively. I'd been through an unsettling divorce after 16 years of marriage and was trying to understand who I really am. In addition, I'd been stuck artistically for many years, unable to paint or create new art. So this message was quite significant to me, and I confess that I was ready to get unstuck and make some major changes.

Another exercise we did in the dream workshop was to write a poem or Haiku about the dream. Here is what I wrote:

REM Ram
Rite of passage dreamed
Old friends left behind
Bound forth spring ram.

Another interesting bit of synchronicity, if you will, is that astrologically, my moon was in Aries, and I had this dream in April, the time period of Aries.

However, this is not the end of the impact this dream had on my life and my creativity. One of the things I wanted to do was to develop a technique to paint my dream images. Up to this point, I had been working in oil paint, which is very thick, tactile, and—to me—very real. I would always get sucked in to the texture of the paint and making things that I paint seem very real and three-dimensional. This approach was not at all suited to the look I wanted for painting dream images. After the dream workshop, I did a small collage of the cave and the ram in one of my painting classes and then put it aside, not recognizing at the time that this small collage foreshadowed a whole new way of creating my art.

A couple of years later, I took a site-specific art class. The objective of the class was for us to go to a specific place for 12 successive weeks and to "respond to the site artistically." The site was an old military bunker in Marin County on San Francisco Bay. We had no assignments, no direction, and no choice of artistic materials to give us guidance. The only directive was that we were supposed to react intuitively and artistically to the site.

So I started out by making small porcelain clay models of my white ram and photographing him in different places at the site. We had hills, weeds, a small rocky beach, and a large concrete slab area to work with.

And then very interesting things started to happen with the models of the ram. He quickly got out of the birth position and stood upright. Then he grew hands, got a partner, and ultimately, dissolved in the waters of the bay only to be reborn.

When I moved up to the concrete slab area of the site, previous artists had spray painted stencils onto the slab. These stencils were abstract shapes. But they gave me the idea to design and cut out a stencil of the ram. First I did one ram, then more rams, and the rams started to change and transmute, getting more elaborate horns and standing up on their hind legs. I designed more stencils that were not rams. One of them was the head of a raging, roaring lion. I sprayed the stencils onto the concrete slab, and the stencils and the clay models of the ram interacted in interesting ways in the photographs. At first, the ram was afraid of the lion, but the fear quickly turned into a partnership.

Then, wanting to work more with the stencils and not to wait until the next class, I started spray painting the stencils onto canvas. Then I took the canvasses to the site and photographed them together with the clay models.

I got a set of small alphabet stencils and began playing around with words that incorporated the word ram in them: rambunctious, ramparts, Ramakrishna, ramifications, drama. I spray painted these words onto the concrete slab and staged scenarios that acted out the words.

Hands are very important, both symbolically and as the tools we use to manifest our creativity. I put hand prints onto many things at the site in honor of aboriginal artists. At this site are huge copper balls that had been used as floats for the nets that were strung underwater to keep submarines out of San Francisco Bay during World War II. These balls are about 6 feet in diameter, rust red where they have been underwater, and a marvelous copper oxide blue-green where they have been exposed to the air. Using some of my pottery glaze chemicals, I alternated copper oxide and iron oxide hands around the perimeter where the colors changed. Of course, the rams got to stand on top of these globes as if they were standing on top of the world.

One of the stencils of a ram had hands sprouting from the top of his head instead of horns. I cut a giant hand, four feet long, from magenta foil and included that in my photographs along with many other elements.

For my final assignment, I sifted through my hundreds of photographs, selected 36 of them, and arranged them in a grid that tells the story of the ram in the cave, from his birth, joining with friends, growing of hands, dealing with fear (the raging red lion), standing on top of the world, playing in the sand, dissolving in the ocean, and re-emerging from the sand reborn.

And still the ram is not done with me, nor I with him. After the class was over, I continued to work with the stencils, because they gave me a flat and surreal look that expressed quite well the dreamy quality I wanted for paintings about dreams. I could also change scale radically from item to item, putting images together in a very dream-like way. I became very proficient with the spray paint and can mix and blend colors on the fly while overlapping the images. I overlap images and then bring part of the underlying image to the front of the canvas again by repositioning the stencil and lightly respraying part of the image.

After I worked with stencils for a while, I decided I wanted to experiment with stencil drawing using the human form. So I made an agreement with a teacher of life drawing to attend her class without having to do the formal exercises. It was in that class that I met my second husband, who is a fabulous model with a physique exactly suited to the stencil technique.

I became fascinated with distilling the human form down to the fewest number of essential shapes, so the figure remains abstract yet very real. The gesture, position, and attitude of the body convey much emotion.

I started cutting these stencils into photographs, many with dream-like double exposures. I worked with the stencils themselves as objects, not as a means to "paint" something, and started to play with layers of paper. I spray painted other stencils onto the glass to provide even more layers.

You can see that, starting with my REM ram, I galloped off in many different creative directions. And the process continues yet.

I tell this story not only to share it with you, but to show that you, too, can work with your dreams to ignite the creative fires. What are the lessons you can learn from my experience?

• Sometimes you have to leave behind old friends and old ideas about how to do things before you can open the door to new ideas.

• You may not always immediately understand the message of a creative dream. That's OK.

• You can (and should) ask for help in interpreting a dream that sticks with you and puzzles you. Ask friends, have a tarot reading, go to a psychic, take a dream workshop, join a dream group, meditate, schedule a hypnotherapy session, ask for another dream that explains the first one.

• You may have to face up to old fears before you can move into the creative realm. When you're resistant to the message of the dream, you're more likely to need help in understanding the message.

- Don't put a time limit on understanding a dream. Sometimes the understanding comes years and years later, at just the right time for you to benefit from it.

- Don't limit your expectations. From just one dream, I've gotten years of kaleidoscopic crea-tivity, a new relationship, and a better under-standing of myself.

- Don't expect all of your dreams to be catalysts to creativity. I'd suggest that you focus on dreams that seem symbolic and stick in your mind. Start working with those dreams you want to share with others because they puzzle or intrigue you.

3

HEALING DREAMS

"LUNACY"

I am at a Halloween party. An acquaintance from work is wearing a big black hat with an enormous floppy brim that is actually an energy net half an inch thick and spongy to the touch. I tell her I have been trying to heal my poison oak by using powers of the *mind and I ask her if she can do it for me with her powers. She says, "Sure" and two beams of light come from the hat onto the two spots on my ankles that are afflicted. Then the poison oak itching starts to come back. She says, "Wait. In an hour it will be gone."*

*Poison Oak Healing
—November 1, 1981*

The night before I had this dream, I got really angry at a three-inch spot of poison oak on my left leg. I didn't think it was right that a stupid plant could cause my body so much discomfort. So I incubated a dream stating my strong desire to get rid of my reaction to poison oak. That night, I had the Poison Oak Healing dream in which an acquaintance (not even a friend) cured me of the symptoms of poison oak.

In the morning when I woke up, the poison oak spot did not itch at all. I said, "I don't believe it," and in the next breath, "Oh, yes, I do!" I didn't want to cancel out the effects of the dream and bring back the horrible itching. In fact, the patch of poison oak looked the same but never itched again. The rash took a couple of weeks to go away, but it never bothered me at all. I have not had poison oak since.

I remember the fabulous feeling of dominion over my body that I felt after I had this dream. I was euphoric. I was really in control. So, I can say from personal experience that you can heal your physical body in your dreams!

Another significant fact of this healing dream is that I asked for help and was willing to receive it. I did not feel I had to do it all by myself.

So, you might well ask, if I can heal myself in my dreams, have I ever been sick in the last 16 years? The answer is yes, of course. Have I healed myself in my dreams again? Never in such a dramatic way. However, I believe that we truly are in charge of our bodies and that we choose any illness we have for a reason. Until we understand the reason, we end up treating just the symptoms.

If you believe as I do that you choose your own illnesses, and that they are a message from some aspect of yourself, then it only makes sense that you can ask other aspects of yourself what the message is and what the condition represents to you. You can ask yourself for information about an illness both in meditation and in your dreams.

And, you can also heal emotional and spiritual wounds in your dreams. I consider the rest of the dreams in this chapter to be healing, although no overt physiological effects were ever observed as a result of them. I believe those dreams that bring us a feeling of overwhelming peace and tranquility are, in fact, healing dreams.

The following dreams have given me that feeling of peace and tranquility, as well as a feeling of personal power. Any dream that reminds you of your own power and place in the universe is profoundly healing, because we all tend to forget how powerful we really are.

The essence of a healing dream is to connect with the truth of who you are, whether the dream be a healing of your body to remind you that you are in charge and responsible for your own destiny or a reminder of your own remarkable powers in other areas.

The diversity and variety of these healing dreams show us that their importance is not in the imagery but in the feelings that they evoke. We carry forward these states of being with us into our waking state.

> *I was at a psychic fair. I told a woman that my aura felt very red. She said I can fix that and worked on cleansing my aura. By the time she was done, I was so relaxed I was lying on the ground. Somehow (maybe the result of the aura cleansing) I could tell who at the fair was fake and who had genuine abilities.*
>
> *Psychic Fair*
> *– November 1981*

In this dream, not only is the red (anger?) cleansed from my aura by virtue of my asking for help, but I am also reminded that I know and can understand the truth and essence of things and that I can tell the difference between fakery and real healing abilities.

I am walking on a path on the beach following a crowd of people. There is nobody behind me. I look out to sea and there are three groups of animals in and above the water. The group on the left is penguins. The one in the middle is big blue swordfish. The group on the right is dolphins. The swordfish are leaping completely out of the water as are the dolphins and penguins. I am trying to photograph them but have the wrong lens on my camera. I keep going farther out in the water to get closer.

There are hundreds of dolphins and penguins and fewer (but still a lot) of the swordfish. Then ships appear on the horizon. Someone says they have come to feed the penguins. With the ships on the horizon, the penguins

*started leaping out of the water
and splashing about. I have a
marvelous feeling of the beauty of
these wild creatures and the abundance of the sea.*

*Dolphins, Penguins, and Swordfish
–May 6, 1987*

This marvelous dream is full of animal life and
exuberance. When I wake, the images that stay with
me are the beauty of these leaping creatures and the
fecundity of nature. In addition, it is not just the sea
that is providing the bounty. Mankind, represented by
the ships that come to feed the penguins, is taking part
in the miracle of life and the abundance of nature. It's
not just nature in its abundance, but the interaction of
mankind with nature that is the message of this dream.
Life is important, as well as the care we take of the
planet and the nurturing of all life upon it.

*I am in a beautiful building with
lots of light and a beautiful star-
shaped cupola in the middle of the
roof. It is like a shaker building,
and there are no interior walls. In
the center of the building is a
small structure that looks like a
simple greenhouse. The city
fathers want me to build a new*

roof for the greenhouse for some
reason that seems to have to do
with keeping the weather out.
However the exterior structure
seems to be watertight.

So the curator explains how
things used to be in the building
and that the knowledge of how the
building functions was lost. As
I look at the rest of the roof (I
was distracted before by the
cupola), I notice a series of
pulleys and cranks that can be
used to move the panels back and
forth to control the light and
temperature in the room.

I show the curator how to unfold
the panels and the whole building
floods with light. Everyone sees
instantly that the inadequate
little greenhouse can be dispensed
with and the purpose of the whole
structure becomes clear once
again.

Opening the Greenhouse
–August 27, 1981

When I woke up, I knew instantly that a rebirth and rediscovery had taken place, and the structure (my body, my spiritual nature) had been limited or been used for completely the wrong function for quite some time because I had forgotten the knowledge of how to use it. I was growing things in my "greenhouse" that occupied only a fraction of the space available to me in the entire building.

This dream started me thinking about how I might have been restricting myself to one small area of experience and expertise. I started thinking about how to expand into all the available beautiful, light-filled space that I had forgotten about. This dream is truly a healing dream in terms of reminding me of the essence of who I am. It woke me up to the idea that light is everywhere and that I could expand and grow in a multitude of different areas that I had not been considering before. A wonderful dream.

> *I dream about a Japanese garden with all kinds of oval shapes, contrasting light and shadows, oval river rocks, but no plants. It is very tranquil and peaceful. I wake up feeling very rested and happy.*
>
> *Japanese Garden*
> *–January 29, 1987*

The important element of this dream is the beauty of the garden and the feeling of peace and tranquility that it brings to me. Waking rested and happy starts my day off on a positive note that carries me forward in a very healing and nurturing way.

> *I am supposed to let go of my anger and wonderful things will happen. I am in a library with stuffed animal heads all over the walls. I let go of my anger and a moose head comes to life and starts munching on papers I hold in my right hand. I can feel the soft warmth of his breath and muzzle on my hand.*
>
> *Stuffed Moose Head*
> *—February 15, 1989*

According to Ted Andrews in his marvelous book *Animal-Speak*, the moose represents primal feminine energies and the magic of life and death. He says, when moose appears in dreams, it reflects a long, good life. At the time I had this dream, I did not know about this interpretation of the spiritual powers of moose energy. I knew only that the moose was a very loving and caring being, and that there was something magical about the feeling of the soft muzzle and its breath on my hand.

And letting go of my anger enabled me to experience this loving and caring being.

The final dream of this chapter is a simple message that came to me as I drifted off to sleep.

> *The line that will help you often lies searching for you.*
>
> *Helping Line*
> *–June 8, 1985*

We frequently make things too hard for ourselves in both the waking and dreaming state. The simple message of this dream or insight is that help is just around the corner. The answers are within yourself. You do not need to expend a tremendous amount of effort in looking for the answers, because the answers are out there looking for you and hoping beyond hope that you will stumble upon them and discover them.

Implicit in this message is another thought. There is nothing wrong in asking for help. In fact, sometimes it is the only answer. Ask and ye shall receive. The more you open yourself to the possibility that the answers, the healing, the cure are out there and available to you, the easier it is for your guides and guardians to provide you with the answers you seek.

And here's another very recent dream with a cogent reminder:

Eric Roberts (the actor) and I are in a car going somewhere. Eric hands me a plate of fried chicken bones. He tells me these are called "mortadellas," which means "little twists of fate." He tells me I should hang onto them because they represent the little ironies of life where things that seem to be bad news end up being good happenings.

Mortadellas
—June 24, 1995

I thought mortadellas might represent "little deaths," but to my surprise, my dictionary says that a mortadella is a sausage seasoned with myrtle. So I looked up myrtle and found that this plant is used as an emblem of love and was anciently held sacred to Venus.

It's amazing what information comes in dreams that turns into fascinating talismans in waking life. In any event, this dream is the clearest one I can ever remember having that says quite clearly that every setback is a new opportunity.

So, pay attention to those dreams that bring you a feeling of well-being, peace, and tranquility. Do not be afraid to ask your dreams to give you answers about your state of health, or the reason for why you might not be as healthy as you think you should be.

If you get messages in your dreams about your health, check them out. The information may be literal or it may be symbolic. If, for example, you dream that your cholesterol level is high, it wouldn't hurt to have some lab work done just to be sure. The message may be symbolic and have nothing to do with your physical body, but it might be a direct communication from your higher self that you need to attend to a physical condition.

Many times dreams about your physical body are symbolic. A specific example is dreaming about being pregnant. Pregnancy dreams, for me, always represent some new project or interest that is gestating and waiting to be born. Sometimes the project is an obvious one and other times it is a more subtle emerging or awakening that is happening in my life.

But it's like having dreams about your car (which frequently, for me, represents my physical body). If I dream I'm running out of gas, or there's a problem with my tires, or some such, the first thing I do is to check on the condition of my car. Sometimes information comes in such a direct way in our dreams that we try to turn it into something else. If the car is fine, if the body is fine, then look to a subtler or more symbolic interpretation. Just don't forget the obvious in your search for symbol and interpretation in your dreams!

If you are interested in taking responsibility for your own health and working with the idea that you can heal yourself in the waking state, I recommend that you get a set of the Lazarus tapes, "Healing: The Nature of Health Part I" and "Healing: The Nature of Health Part II." I have had much success in healing myself of conditions such as food allergies and menstrual cramps by working with the process Lazarus suggests.

4

GREAT TEACHERS

"DARK POWER"

I am working on an archaeological dig in a sacred temple. Joe Montana is one of the workers. We are putting the pieces together and reconstructing and reconnecting the temple so people can worship properly again. Joe and I move a big sandstone slab carved with runes and symbols into a niche in the wall where it belongs, and put a statue in its proper place in front of the slab.

Reconstructing the Sacred Temple
–September 22, 1995

I was taking a class to learn how to do hypnotherapy, and I had this dream the morning after doing my very first, and very successful, hypnotherapy session with a co-worker. Why was Joe Montana in this dream, and why did I choose it to introduce this chapter? I believe that Joe Montana is one of the great teachers of our time, and that the great teachers are not only those figures like Buddha, Christ, or Mother Theresa. Joe Montana is living the true karmic life. He did what he knew best and made it look easy. He loved what he did and had fun with it. He made others around him believe they could do the same. Whenever he played football, his example inspired his teammates to elevate their level of play as much as possible to match his.

The message of this dream is to confirm that, just as Joe Montana was fulfilling his karmic destiny by being a great quarterback, I am on the right track with pursuing hypnotherapy as a way to enable people to solve their problems and move into their own power.

I believe each person has a powerful set of spirit guides and guardian angels just chomping at the bit to provide help. These guides and guardians are energies or beings who are not, at the moment, inhabiting a physical body. They are, however, part of your karmic family and continue to feel the connection and the bond. Your guides and guardians are always there willing and ready to help. You are the one that "goes away" by not paying attention to messages or by discounting them as coincidence when they do come. However, asking for their help directs your guides to the areas where you are blocked. Asking for help also opens yourself up and you become more receptive to help when it arrives.

Other teachers can also influence you. These teachers are people in your life whom you admire, or who cause you trouble in a way that makes you look more closely at yourself and your patterns. They also might be famous people who embody attributes you react strongly to, whether in a positive or a negative way.

Our spirit guides and teachers come to us in dreams. Sometimes we don't recognize them. Sometimes their presence is so obvious that we can't fail to get the message. When you dream about famous people, they can represent messages from your higher self or from your guides and guardians. Because you are not receptive to hearing disembodied voices while you are awake, and sometimes do not trust messages that you receive in your meditations, your guides and guardians frequently give you messages in your dreams.

Throughout my life, I have had countless wonderful spiritual dreams, as well as dreams about great teachers and role models. Even when I had not yet begun my spiritual path, I had these dreams. I believe this was the way my teachers used to ask me to wake up and become more conscious.

> *I dream I am in a cave in India where there are gigantic statues of the Buddha carved out of the living rock. A throng is gathered on the floor of the cavern and another group of people stands on the stone balcony above. Someone does a channeling for the group. Then a friend of mine does one. Then they turn to me and say, "It's your turn now." I am quite surprised and unprepared because I am part of the entourage. But I say, "Well, OK." I go into a trance and slump over the stone parapet. I hear myself begin to channel information about the Buddha, love, and light. And then I go completely unconscious. When I come to (in the dream) I am lying on my back on the flagstones and someone is standing*

*over me handing me a small black
leather-bound book that contains
the teachings I have channeled.*

*Channeling the Buddha
—June 17, 1987*

In the Channeling the Buddha dream, the cave in India is a sacred place. I think I'm there as an observer, and I definitely feel the energy and importance of the place. And suddenly I'm called to step forward to take my place as an important part of the ritual. Even though I feel unprepared (and perhaps a little unworthy), I do my part. And my reward for this participation is a book containing the information that I channeled as part of the dream.

When I started channeling in September, 1986, by sitting down at a computer screen and typing what came into my head, one of the first communications was about dreams:

*You have been listening to us
with your dreams for a long, long
time. And very consciously so.
Our messages through the dreams
have been getting clearer and
clearer. Don't you remember the
dream of everyone walking around
as light beings with little rents in*

their physical essence, letting the inner light shine out? That's as clear a message as you have ever received, and it was not in the least bit encrypted. That is why you have had fewer and stronger dreams.

Channeled Message
–September 1986

The Channeling the Buddha dream was a strong message telling me that even though I did not think I was ready (or worthy), it was time for me to accept these gifts and talents. So, if you're interested in channeling information from your guides and guardians, paying attention to the teachers in your dreams is an excellent way to get connected. Another message of the Channeling the Buddha dream is that the channel is still open and available to me to tap into whenever I choose.

Here's another dream with Buddha imagery:

My husband and I are with a group of people in a boat. We are going out to an amusement island. We arrive at the dock which is a roofed structure. There is a narrow walkway out into the tumultuous ocean. Part of the

group wants to go out that way,
and my husband is part of that
group. I decide to stay with the
children on the platform because I
know I would be afraid and fall
off the narrow path. The group
starts out the path and I then
notice that the path is made of
giant floating bronze footprints.
The first people who step onto the
footprints are slipping and
laughing and falling in the water.
I am glad I decided to stay
behind. The children are laughing
and giggling and we are having a
good time. They feel more secure
having an adult with them, and I
am pleased to be there. The texture of the feet is beautiful and
the copper green is vivid and
lovely in the frothing water.

Footprints of Buddha
- December 8, 1987

The message of this dream is that it is possible for
individuals to follow their own truth or path. Not
everyone needs to walk the slippery path out into the
dashing waves to enjoy the footprints. I had the Buddha

dream as part of an exercise I was doing in a certification class for reading Voyager Tarot®. The exercise was to do a reading and then have a dream that would interpret the reading. This dream was my interpretation of a tarot reading, and one of the cards in the reading was the Hierophant. In the Voyager deck, the Hierophant is represented by the Buddha.

Kwan Yin is the Chinese goddess of mercy and compassion. I had the following dream the morning after a workshop session in which we experienced a guided meditation to connect with the energies of Kwan Yin.

> *I'm walking across the face of a giant statue lying on its back in a field of tall grass. I realize the statue is of Kwan Yin.*
>
> *Kwan Yin*
> *–August 23, 1993*

During the meditation, I could feel Kwan Yin's energies, but could not see her. Other members of the group had vivid visual images, and although I know that's not my way of experiencing things in these circumstances, I was disappointed and a bit jealous of the visions that other members of the group had. So, of course, in my own way by using my dreams I found a way to complete the exercise to my satisfaction.

I am at a computer conference in Afghanistan. A bus comes. It's a typical Indian bus with fringes, icons, and idols all over the windshield. We're sitting in the back of the bus, which is open like the tailgate of a truck. We're facing backward, looking at the way we have come. A woman in the back of the bus says we're just going to lunch.

The bus goes to a restaurant. I'm looking for familiar faces but don't recognize anyone. I wander into an auditorium where there's a lecture going on about moving the remains of Elvis to a sacred cave.

I realize I know these caves, which are in India. I go to the caves. I've been there before. The images of Christian symbolism are all covered with writings in Hindi and symbols of Om in very bright and beautiful colors. I go to the end of the cave and see the

*place where they plan to put
Elvis's remains.*

*I don't see the remains, but I am
aware of somebody standing a
little behind me and to the left,
and I can see that the legs of this
person are dressed in gold lame. I
know, somehow, that these are
Elvis's remains.*

*Elvis's Remains
–July 20, 1993*

I got a good laugh out of this dream. For some, Elvis is
considered a sacred symbol, but I don't feel that way
about him. At the time I had this dream, the company
I worked for was planning for a major computer conference. So that's where that part came from. In waking
life, I have been to India, but not to sacred caves. And
I have never been to Afghanistan. In my personal belief
system, I have problems with organized Christian
religions. I do, however, believe that Christ, along with
Buddha and Mohammed and others, was a great teacher.
Historically, the Christian religion tried to overlay or
suppress older, more pagan religions. So the obscuring
of Christian symbols with the older symbols of the
Hindu religions seems an easy and natural thing to me.

Although I had lots of fun telling my friends about my Elvis's Remains dream, I have not yet figured out what message Elvis may have had for me.

> *I dream about a Native American spirit crossing over to be with me as a "new" guide and also about studying at the "youniversity" of life.*
>
> New Guide
> –March 7, 1994

I had this dream about a new guide on the morning of my 51st birthday. I already knew that I had several Native American guides and was glad to welcome this one into my ever-expanding spiritual family. And, a few weeks later, I had another dream that showed the influence of my new guide.

> *I hear a Native American chanting the ways, telling stories of encounters with bear, eagle, snake, and so on. He is chanting in a language that I can understand, although it is not a language that I know.*
>
> Chanting the Ways
> –April 22, 1994

How can you recognize great teachers in your dreams?

First, I would suggest that you open your heart and mind to the possibility that your guides and guardians can and do use your dreams as teaching tools.

Then I suggest that you ask them to send you information, not only through your dreams, but through whatever means are appropriate.

When you have dreams about people you know, famous or otherwise, ask yourself what you admire about them. Look for a possible message from someone you recognize communicated through your dream.

Also ask yourself what you do not like about certain people in your dreams. Look at why you do not like them, and consider how you might be similar to them. You may be expressing yourself in ways that match these people, without even realizing it.

Sometimes the great teacher dreams are easy and obvious to interpret. The Reconstructing the Sacred Temple dream at the beginning of this chapter had a feeling, a meaning, and an interpretation that was immediately obvious to me. My reaction was, "Of course. Thanks for the validation and feedback."

And yet, I still do not understand the message of the Elvis's Remains dream. It may take me years before I get it, or I may never understand what it means. It might have been simply an entertainment, although the energy of those sacred caves in India was powerful and intense.

Play with the ideas of these dreams. Share them with others. But do not let somebody else tell you what the dream means, unless their interpretation feels absolutely right to you. And if you dream about somebody like Dom Deluise, only you know whether you consider him a bumbling fool or a gifted comic.

5

OUR ANIMAL ALLIES

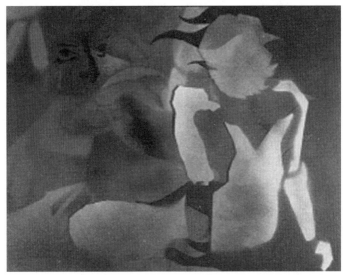

"CREATIVITY"

*The ocean is as smooth as glass
and a silvery blue-gray color.
And it is full of snakes, except
instead of swimming in the ocean,
they are moving across the top of
it as though it is a plate of glass.*

There are tiny snakes no bigger than a pencil and huge snakes as big around as my arm. I see the palm trees on an island off to my right and realize that, in my fascination with the snakes, I have swum miles from my destination. I start to swim towards the island. I look for whales and dolphins, but I don't see any.

Later after I am on the island, I see a bay full of breaching humpback whales and frolicking dolphins. I am thrilled at the sight.

Ocean of Snakes
–October 10, 1994

I had this dream when I was going through major life transformations. I had separated from my second husband and was trying to move the relationship on to the next phase, and I was just about to start a new job. For me, the snakes represent transformation. Not only were they transformative in and of themselves, they were moving in a very magical and unnatural way across the ocean. And whales and dolphins represent the essence of who I am.

We all have animal allies that are here to guide and protect us, as well as to give us information and act as lessons. For example, we could all learn lessons from our pets. Cats and dogs do not have hidden agendas. They tell us when they are hungry, when they need to relieve themselves, and when they crave affection. But animal allies are special animals that are usually symbolic in some way. That's not to say that our pets cannot be our animal friends. It's quite likely that they are.

I asked my dreams one time to tell me who my guardian angels were. The answer was my three cats: Wee Too, Pee Wee, and Magic. Once I started watching how they behaved and how they interacted with me, it became obvious how they are watching out for me, especially when I'm sleeping.

I have a long list of animal allies, although it was not until the past few years that I have become connected to them consciously. Just a few of my animals are whales, dolphins, snakes, frogs, a big male lion, my three cats, rams, and ravens.

You can connect with your animals both symbolically and literally. Today, I had a marvelous, conscious encounter with dolphins, one of my animal allies. I am fortunate enough to be able to work at my home in Half Moon Bay two days a week. After a morning of sitting at my computer working on writing a software manual, I suddenly felt the urge to go for a walk on the beach. The day was gray, drizzly, and overcast, so it wasn't the bright sunshine that called me.

I bundled up and went out the back gate, through the field that belongs to the California State Park, across the Coastside trail, across the bridge over Pilarcitos Creek, and down to the beach. This pleasant walk is about a quarter of a mile. As I walked toward the ocean, I scanned the water, as is my custom, to see what birds and animals were around.

And right in front of me, I saw a fin slicing through the waves. It vanished immediately, and I wondered if I had imagined it. This year, I have not seen any dolphins in Half Moon Bay. The dolphins come here infrequently, and I cherish the encounters.

Yes, it was a fin, and there were two others. Three dolphins were swimming north at about a walking pace, just outside the surf line, fairly close to shore. I thanked the universe for this marvelous gift and started pacing the dolphins as they swam. We moved together about a mile and a half down the beach. Then I said to them, "I have to turn back soon. It would be wonderful if you would turn around and swim back with me." I had no expectations that they would hear my request, but I figured it was worth a try. A few minutes later, the dolphins swam in a circle for a few minutes and then turned and started moving south.

"Wow," I said. "Thanks. That's really neat." As I watched them swim and surface, I was startled to notice a fourth, tiny fin in the pod. I wasn't sure I was really seeing it, but kept watching and walking. As I returned to the path back to my house, I stopped and stood on the beach. The dolphins turned in a circle, and started swimming back up the beach again. Just as they were leaving, I clearly saw that there was, indeed, a fourth, newborn dolphin among the group. I felt very blessed to have been present at the birth of a baby dolphin!

Was it just synchronicity between my movements and the movements of the pod, or were the dolphins tuned in to my energies and willing to share the gift of the birth with me? Who's to say. All I know is that it is a magical memory that will stay with me.

What does it mean when you dream about animals? Each person's animal symbology is unique. You are the only one who can determine what dreaming about a particular animal means to you.

However, if you're interested in other interpretations, many books are available that discuss the symbolic spiritual and magical powers of animals. To mention a few, Jamie Sams has written a wonderful book and has created "Medicine Cards" that discusses the spiritual energies of animals according to the Native American traditions. Ted Andrews' book, *Animal-Speak*, provides a comprehensive dictionary of animal, bird, and reptile symbolism. The Zuni tribe has a strong tradition of connection to animal energies and believe that rocks resembling these animals, called fetishes, are the embodiment of such energies. The Zuni feed, talk to, and share breath with their animal fetishes. In the last 15 years, Zuni fetishes have become widely available.

Hal Zina Bennett's book, *Zuni Fetishes*, explains the Zuni symbolism for many of the animals (see bibliography).

If you resonate with a particular animal, you might want to consult one or more of these books for interpretations of the animal energy to help you understand your animal symbol. According to the "Medicine Cards," the dolphin represents manna, the breath of life, and teaches us how to release emotions through dolphin breath. Whales represent the record keeper, the connection to the Akashic Records, the master records of everything that has ever occurred since the beginning of the universe. Snake represents transmutation and the life-death-rebirth cycle.

You can discover your animal allies through your dreams, through meditations, and through your natural connection to these animals. One of the first animals that identified itself to me in my dreams was the dream ram that I discussed in the chapter on Creativity. Once I realized that the ram was one of my animal allies, I looked around my house and found that I had a number of sculptures, paintings, and images representing the ram. At some unconscious level, I knew about the ram and had already incorporated much of the symbolism into the artwork I had in my home.

I have a friend who had a raccoon come to her in a meditation and tell her that he was there to protect her from having other people steal her power. Everyone knows what clever animals raccoons are and how they steal things and get into places other animals can't with their clever little hands. She already understood the symbology of this animal by the time the animal told her why he was there.

One way you can work with the animals that come to you in dreams is to ask them who they are and what they represent. The answers you get from these dialogs with yourself are the true answers. If your animal tells you what it symbolizes and why it's there to help you, it doesn't make any difference what reference books have to say on the subject. Your animal knows its purpose.

> *I am on a camping trip out in the bush. A big male lion is hanging around. I am moving very slowly so he will not attack me. I lie down on the bed and he comes and stretches out next to me with his head near my hand. I slowly put out my hand and touch his nose. Then I scratch him under his neck. When he gets up, the bed smells like lion. My partner comes over and sees the lion. Then another couple comes, and their young boy climbs all over the lion with no fear.*
>
> *Then the lion sits up in an arm-chair like a person. I want to take*

*its picture, but I am concerned
that the flash might startle him.*

*Lion in My Bed
–October 19, 1993*

When I woke up with this dream, I had feelings of awe for the strength of the lion, yet also fear because of his size. I wanted to be with him, but not to take advantage of him. It was a wonderful feeling to be able to connect with the wild energy and deep feelings of respect. This dream was a great gift in granting me permission to connect with my own wild and untamed nature and to realize that I could experience this energy without gobbling up those around me.

I've had lion energy protecting me for many, many years. One of the first animal sculptures I bought was a ceramic male lion. It's possible that this lion energy goes back to the lion Aslan in the marvelous C. S. Lewis books, *The Chronicles of Narnia*, that I was so entranced with as a teenager. Another one of my favorite books at that time was Elizabeth Gouge's *A Little White Horse*. This book also had animal allies for the characters and one of them was a big dog named Rolf, except that he was actually a lion. They called him a dog because they didn't want people to be afraid of the lion.

In fact, I bought a big stuffed lion one day for no apparent reason. At the time, I'd kind of forgotten about my lion energy and my subconscious mind just took over. This stuffed lion now sits on top of one of the bookshelves in my bedroom and guards me while I sleep.

I've also seen this lion many, many times in my meditations and in my dreams. No words, just the picture of the face of a huge lion.

A few years ago, I took a psychic apprenticeship class. One of the class exercises was to connect with our animal allies. In a guided meditation, we were asked to allow our animal allies to show themselves to us. Although I'm an artist, and am very visual, I usually do not see things in meditations or in guided visualizations. However, in this one I did. I saw my male lion, my little white ram from the creativity dream, and the enormous eye of a humpback whale.

I have felt very connected to whales for quite some time, but from the time of this experience the whale has been coming on stronger and stronger. I now realize, from working with the whale energy, from dreams, and from hypnotherapy sessions that I was, in fact, a humpback whale in a former life.

I dream about a beautiful dark brown horse running free from right to left. His mane and tail are flying. He looks like Rising Star, the horse in the movie The Electric Horseman. He's happy but there is a shadow or something vague worrying him.

Dark Horse
–July 24, 1993

The horse is another of my animal allies. The horse represents power. One of my ongoing lessons is learning to be myself and express my own opinions without being afraid of how they affect other people. At this time in my life, I was in the middle of a very political situation at work and I was not being valued for my talents and contributions. Somehow I was being perceived as a threat by others. This dream is a reflection of those energies. Although I want to be a beautiful horse running wild and free, there's something troubling going on.

> *A little green grass snake is keeping me company throughout the night. I am sitting in an amphitheater with a bunch of people and he keeps crawling over me and going down to wrap himself around my right foot.*

Green Grass Snake
–July 10, 1989

This dream is yet another visit from the green grass snake. I don't remember what was happening in my life when I had this dream, but I must have been in yet another period of transition. That's usually when the snakes show up for me.

Here's a long and very involved dream that combines the Akashic Records with a complete cast of animals, many of whom I've never dreamed about before.

> *I am on a plantation with a room that gives people life experiences that teach them to heal themselves. I dream the complete history of the place and who has passed through it. At one point, the room invites all the "keepers" in and then it apparently becomes abandoned. A young vagrant comes and lives by himself in the house for a year, without even knowing about the room.*
>
> *The room has a final lesson to teach about animals. A skunk is frustrated. I wander through a complicated maze. The skunk is building something. Someone is concerned about the deteriorating quality of the structure and takes me to see. Big beams are set in with facings that don't match and boards that are cheap and tacky.*

We find the skunk and ask him what is bothering him. He says, "All of the animals respect me except the otter." We position a yellow portal so that it allows access to an undersea universe with huge beautiful fish. Our mission is to keep the room central to lessons for beings 104—human beings—but we realize that the instruction is very restrictive.

We explain to the skunk that the reason the otter does not respect him is because of his smell. He pollutes the water making the otter think the water is bad, and the smell masks the warmth of the skunk's animal body, which the otter would respect and value as any other animal being.

At the end of the dream, an envelope arrives that contains a card from one of the former visitors to the plantation. It is an appreciation and also a promotion/advertisement for a science fiction book that is the published story these

beings experienced while they were
in the room.

Animal Plantation
–July 16, 1987

The plantation is a place for both humans and animals to learn about tolerance, understanding, and life lessons. And beings 104—human beings—are just another animal species.

How can you connect to your animal allies, and how can they help you?

- Pay attention to animals you dream about. Ask yourself what each animal symbolized for you, whether the animal is a friend or foe. What message does it bring? What is the animal's name? The name can be symbolic or literal. What does the name tell you?

- Look around your house. Your animal allies may already be represented in paintings or sculptures, or in the kinds of books that attract you.

- Ask your animal allies to come to you in meditations and dreams and give you messages or help you through difficult situations.

- Notice which animals that attract your attention. If you always notice the hawks, for example, hawk may be one of your animal allies.

- Your animal allies can help you simply to recon-
nect with the world of nature. If you feel drawn to
sea otters, as I was for many years, you're more
likely to go to the Monterey, CA area. If you're
drawn to whales, a trip to Maui in the spring or a
whale watching expedition elsewhere may break
up the monotony and get you out of ruts. If you're
drawn to marmots, a trip to the Yosemite high
country or to the Alabama Hills behind Mt.
Whitney may be in order.

- Your animals can also help you symbolically. If
your animal ally is the rabbit, for example, he can
help you master your fears. Work with the concepts suggested in some of the books about spiritual symbolism of animals. Be careful, however,
not to mask or hide your own interpretation and
feeling about the message of your animal just
because someone else says it means something
different. You are always right about what your
animals symbolize to you!

- Do some research on the life habits and patterns
of your animal allies. See if some habit or pattern
from these animals manifests itself somehow in
your life.

6

PAST LIVES

"DREAMTIME"

My husband and I are living in
New Zealand. We are in an
isolated area with lots of red rock
formations. The building we live
in is constructed totally of rust
colored brick—floors, walls,
ceilings, inside and out. The
rooms are huge and cavernous

with 30-foot-high ceilings. I suppose that the brick will be easy to clean because of the pervasive red dust. We have two daughters, about 7 and 8. They are quiet, slight, with long straight blond hair. At the end of the dream I am lying, on my back, outside in the dirt with aboriginal paintings all over my nude body. My arms are stretched out beside me and my eyes are closed. I can feel the pulsing of the energy of the earth and see rainbows of color as I am connected to the marvelous energy of mother earth.

New Zealand
—May 17, 1989

I have never lived in New Zealand, nor have I been there. I have no children. To me, this dream has much of the feeling of a past life. Some years later, as I worked with information about my past lives in workshops and hypnotherapy sessions, I realized that I have had many past lives as an Australian aborigine. These lives may be my direct connection to the importance of dreams and to the Australian aboriginal concept of the dream time. In fact, I later remembered this dream as taking place in Australia, and did a painting of it titled

Dreamtime. It may be that at first I was slightly displaced geographically and that this dream was really of Australia, or I may have had past lives as a Maori in New Zealand as well.

In any event, my past-life connection to this dream is not important as merely a curiosity, or a way of saying I lived then or there, or I was that person. It is important when the information it conveys is relevant to my experiences in this lifetime.

I believe that we have lived in other times and other places. Have you ever gone to a new place and had a deja vu feeling that you knew the place and had been there before? Have you ever met a complete stranger and felt that you have been old friends and known one another for a long time? Have you ever consistently called an acquaintance or a friend by the wrong name? I believe these are examples of memories our souls and our cells hold of other lives we have led.

In working with dreams and, more recently for me, with hypnotherapy, both as a client and as a therapist, past lives come up over and over again. Are they real? To me they are. Many examples have been documented that the past lives people remembered—consciously, through hypnotic past life regression, or through dreams—can be confirmed. However, regardless of whether or not you believe past lives are real, they work very effectively as metaphor. If the dream is meaningful to you, it conveys something—an emotion, a message, a feeling—that is relevant to you in this lifetime.

I have many dreams of strange places and familiar people out of their normal context. I have wakened with a word from another language in my head. When I write it down and look it up, or ask about it, the word invariably is in a language that I do not know, and it is always relevant to the dream I've experienced. I have dreamed Chinese characters, written them down, and had them translated for me. Instead of being nonsense, they always make perfect sense.

The explanation that works for me is that these are fragments from other lives that I am remembering through my dreams.

> I am the Dali Lama. The old Lama has died and I am to continue the chain of reincarnations. Lots of bald-headed Tibetans in saffron robes, caves, and so on. One of the things I must do to preserve the lineage is to eat the mummified remains of the old Lama. It is a small body that fits on the palm of my hand. I start with the head, grimacing a little at the idea, but the taste is sweet.
>
> Dali Lama
> –August 6, 1991

When I had this dream, I dreamed it over and over and over and over that night. It is as if I was experiencing the complete chain of reincarnations, all in the same dream. I don't remember what was happening in my life at the time, but I did feel the sacred energy of the Dali Lama and the weight of memories and history of the Tibetan people. This dream had a strong impact on me and I do remember that the feelings and emotions from it stayed with me for many weeks.

I have a series of dreams of past life experiences in tribal Africa. Botswana? And I am there in a dual role, as a tribal member and as a tour guide. I have a camera and take pictures but the back of the camera opens as I am showing someone else how to rewind the film, and it is ruined.

But when I take the film to the camera store, they can develop it. When I pick up the photos, the images are visible, but over time they disappear. Some of the photos are excellent. One is a close-up of two tribesmen with mud-caked masks. Several are excellent shots of a tribal dance where the men are leaping into the

*air. The photos caught the bodies
in mid air and the shadows on the
ground look like lizards and
snakes. In one of the photos, I
can see a trampoline in the lower
right corner. I didn't remember the
trampoline from when I was
taking the photos, just the leaping
bodies.*

*Fading Photos
—August 8, 1993*

I dream of tribal Africa quite frequently, and I do believe I've had many lifetimes there. I had always wanted to go to Africa, and when I finally went to Kenya for a photo safari in August of 1988, I had a total feeling of coming home. I remember my first husband telling me of a trip that he and his second wife took to Jamaica, and how for the first time he felt uncomfortable being in the racial minority. So, I had wondered if I would have a similar feeling in Africa. Quite to the contrary, even though I was a white woman in Africa, I felt completely at home both with the landscape and with the people.

*I am an African storyteller
learning the importance of
cadence, rhythm, and repetition
in the telling of stories.*

I am in Africa at a festival for
the spring equinox. I am not
African but a tourist. I wander
through the festival and see an
African psychic giving readings.
I ask if she will read for me. She
says, "No, because you need an
appointment, but also because
you already know the answers."

I wander some more and wonder
that I can understand the language they are speaking. I find
another mystic giving readings. I
wait. After she completes the
reading, she comes over to me and
asks, "Did you see me looking at
you?" I had not noticed. I ask if
she will read for me and she says,
"No, because you already know
what to do."

I wander some more and come to
a third reader. I wait patiently
and ask her if she will read for
me. She also says no and tells me
that I should be reading for her.

African Psychics
—April 14, 1992

I had these two dreams in quick succession one night. In the first dream, I am an African woman. In the second, I am a tourist in Africa. At the time, I was trying to decide whether I felt sufficient self-confidence in my tarot readings to begin charging for them. Both these dreams address the issue I was working on. Tarot readings are a form of storytelling. In fact, frequently when I do readings, I'll say, "This is the story the cards are telling you." I found it fascinating that my answer to this question came from Africa in two dreams. The second one more directly addresses the issue and is a definite confirmation that I am capable and should be doing readings. I like the fairy-tale-like three times that the question is asked and then answered, each time a little more fully.

Past lives are not only about places you have lived, but also about people you have known. I have had countless dreams of being in unusual places with people whom I see and interact with in my everyday life. Many times people who are only casual acquaintances in this life time show up in the strangest and sometimes most intimate circumstances. I usually look at these dreams as conveying information about this person, about how I relate to him or her, or how I feel. If the dream itself gives me new hints and insights that are useful, although they could be indications of a past-life connection, I don't necessarily consider that to be the strongest component of the dream. And some dreams have such a strong feeling of connection and familiarity that I believe they are.

It's fun to consider the past-life connections we have with people and places, and possibly of famous people we might have been. For example, I once dreamed I was Eleanor of Aquitaine. Most of the time, except for the Dali Lama, my past lives are ordinary lives of ordinary people.

I suggest you consider the possibility that some of your dreams are about past lives. Please don't get too carried away with the idea and attribute everything to past-life connections. If you are open to the idea and the possibility, over time, I think you'll be able to make your own decisions about what may be a past life and what may be a metaphor or other message from your higher self.

Here are some things to help you evaluate whether a dream might be about a past life:

- Do you dream about a time or a place you've always been drawn to?

- Do these times or places seem familiar to you in your dreams, as though you've been there many times before?

- Do you dream about a person that you know in this lifetime that takes place in an unfamiliar context?

- Do you dream about a person you know in this lifetime that takes place in an unfamiliar relation- ship with you?

- Are you dreaming that you are a famous person?

- Are you dreaming about a job you have never held?

- Do you have recurring dreams about a particular time and place? For example, my recurring dreams about tribal Africa set the stage. When I was told in a psychic reading that I had many past lives in tribal Africa, I said, "Of course."

- Do you dream of technical expertise you do not have. For example, do you dream you are a composer when you think you have little musical talent in this lifetime?

- Do you dream in languages you do not know in your waking state?

7

CHANNELING

"Past Lives"

I am talking to a friend about channeling. She takes me to a reading room in a library where there are all kinds of books of channeled information. She is interested in one entity called Bathar. She shows me how to fill out the chit and turn it in. Then she hands me a leather-bound book that is the first in the series. I leave the library with it and then decide to go back in and read it there. I pass through many halls to go back to the room and as I walk through the halls, the book transforms into a Time-Life book that I know I already own.

I open the book and start to read the words but do not understand them. Then an adjustment is made, a focusing, a tuning in of the level of consciousness, and the information is clear, lucid and obvious, although it is presented in an archaic form and language style.

Then I am at a street fair run by a religious group like the Rosicrucians. They are trying to induce people to channel. They are dressed in tattered clothes and have long matted hair. They have an altar and are burning candles and incense. They light a particularly pungent chunk and hold it up to my nose and start to chant. I go into a trance and am dancing and cavorting with them. "Try it now!" they shout, and I say, "But I'm already channeling Fred." But I try anyhow.

The first thing that happens is that I see a big purple spot that represents Fred. Then the color turns into a kaleidoscopic set of circles about two inches in diameter. They whirl and twirl and I go into a deeper trance. They lead me to a room filled with tables. There is a lot of pottery, most of it with a mottled blue and purple glaze. I know I am in trance and am at about the age of 6. Although I know I should have a "connection" to the pottery, I am in a childish snit. I pick up one bowl that looks like mine, but it isn't. I go around the room looking for the thing I need.

All I see are more and more tables of ceramics.

There is a lady behind a table that has a banner on sticks stretched across it. She says, "Find what you need?" And I say, "No." What I really need is something soft with music and colors. "I have the perfect thing," she says. And out of the cupboard overhead (which had just been a banner before) she pulls a box. When she pulls it off the shelf it looks like a small stuffed cow made of yellow flowered dimity. But when she puts it on the counter it becomes a small rectangular box. There are components you can put together to make different things. There are 4 glass lozenge shaped pieces, green, red, blue, and yellow. And each color has a tone associated with it. You can assemble these in a matrix, constructing anything you wanted from the components. It is delicate and intricate and wonderful.

*I clutch it to my heart and leave
extremely happy.*

*Glass Matrix
–February 3, 1987*

In September of 1986, I started channeling by doing automatic writing. A friend of mine wanted to channel, and she had successfully used this technique a few months earlier. Her spirit guide told her to call him Teacher. I called mine Fred, with his permission, of course. Fred has always been my name for the great unknowable and unknown, so it seemed the right name.

When I was doing the automatic writing, I would see a big purple spot that represented Fred, even though my eyes were open and I was typing on a computer keyboard. I also see this big purple spot when I meditate or when I'm in a hypnotic trance.

Channeling is an interesting experience. If you believe, as I do, that we have a host of spirit guides and guardians willing to help us learn our lessons and live our lives, then why not talk directly to them and allow them to talk directly to us? I believe we receive messages from our guides and guardians in many ways—obviously through our dreams, through synchronicity and coincidence, through seemingly chance encounters with the perfect person for the moment.

I did not have dreams about the channeling experience before I started channeling, but I certainly did during and afterwards in the Glass Matrix dream. I believe these dreams were part of learning to trust the information and the experience.

When I first started channeling, I had lots of questions about whether the experience was real and the information genuine. In many ways, it was like myself talking to myself, telling me things that I already knew and partially understood. However, the style of the channeling was not mine, nor was the extensive use of metaphor.

Consider the following example of channeled information about crystals:

> *There is much to be learned from the crystalline life forms on this planet. They have a sentience, a wisdom, and a knowledge that is quite different from that of the entities that are called human. Because they did not evolve from a splitting of entities into two halves, resulting in a conflict and a battle throughout time between separateness and the joining of these natures, they have a different perception of reality.*
>
> *They have a slow and growing type of wisdom. Theirs is the*

wisdom of knowing who they are,
how they grew, and how the lattice
nature of their essence came into
being. A crystal knows before it is
through growing how big it will
become and what form it will take.
It grows to exactly the right size
and then stops. It does not have
delusions of grandeur. It does
not desire to take over the planet.
It also has a fundamental understanding of its place in the scheme
of things.

Crystals can be used for healing,
for meditation, and to enhance the
natural energy fields of these
entities called human. They can
work with you and for you to
enhance your own abilities. You
can gaze into them and see worlds
and universes beyond your comprehension.

Isn't it amazing how diverse
nature is in the beautiful forms
that it creates for the contem-
plation of you living, sentient
entities on earth's surface.

*Consider that, deep in the bowels
of the earth, even now minerals
are congregating, crystallizing,
forming themselves into glorious
castles of mineral beauty. Spires
and arches, when brought to the
surface, reflect the glorious sun-
light and radiance of the planet in
all directions around them.*

*Crystal Channeling
—September 20, 1986*

And, a few days later, here is what Fred had to share about dreams and dream doors:

*How did you enjoy the dreams we
sent you last night? Weren't they
wonderful? You should, perhaps,
try to write them down so they do
not get lost. But you already
know this. Each dream is an
experience, a transportation to
another dimension, another kind of
reality. They are to be cherished,
enjoyed, pondered, picked up and
reexamined from time to time, as
you might pick up a crystal and
look at the different facets that it*

presents to you. In this way you can experience the fullest understanding of those things that you intuitively grasp.

Your perception of your own particular dream world is quite profound. You have understood the importance of the communications from the dream state much more, and much earlier than have other physical entities. Your work with the dreams and your interpretations of your own particular dream vocabulary have given you a solid grounding on which to build further growth and comprehension.

And yet, now that you start to understand what your dreams have been saying to you, interpreting them as messages from yourself and not from others, you are having to reevaluate the entire experience. Because you are beginning to realize that not only are dreams a method of communicating information from your

inner being or your higher self.
They are a communication on
many different levels and exist
simultaneously on many different
planes of existence.

You have experienced, in recent
months, that your dreams have
been accurate perceptions of
events that were happening in
others' lives. You have also
experienced dreams as a method
of communication between entities
not of this physical existence.
You are beginning to lose con-
fidence in your ability to interpret
dreams because you viewed them
for so long as a communication
with yourself.

They are still that, but there are
other doors opening in the process.
And in fact, some of the communication in the past, the tran-
scendental dreams, have been a
direct connection to the life force
of the universe, to all other entities, as you are a drop of water,
one of many drops inhabiting the

great ocean of human existence.
So you have always known that
the dreams were a "door to elsewhere." You accepted those
important dreams as such a
communication, and were grateful for their gift of information.

We understand that you have
been confused recently about
whether dreams are manifes-
tations of your own wants and
desires, or whether they are an
indication of what is actually
happening on some level of reality.
They can be both. But we sense
that your anxiety dreams will
diminish as you allow the doors to
open onto the other facets of the
universe that you can explore in
this manner.

You are thinking in the manner of
"doors" such as in the book called
The Lion, the Witch, and the
Wardrobe, where the youngsters
exited from the back of the wardrobe into different places, different realities. That is very much

*like what the "dream doors" can
do for you. This is a time of
great change, growth, and transition for you. It will manifest
itself in the way you dream, the
way you react to dreams, and the
way you interact with those
around and about you.*

*Enjoy this change. Revel in it.
Dive through it like Scrooge
McDuck dives through his
money. Continue to share these
experiences, even though they may
seem weird to you. You did, in
fact, shift to a "skunkless reality" in the middle of the night.
And wasn't it easy? You can, as
you become more proficient,
change waking reality with that
much ease and unconscious
grace.*

*Dream Door Channeling
–September 24, 1986*

And, all this time, I thought the title for this book was
my own creation. Ten years ago, Fred gave me the
information, so the credit for the title of this book, and

many of the ideas in it, belong to a discorporate entity! Thanks, Fred.

I'd better explain about the shift to a "skunkless reality." The garbage cans were right outside the bedroom of the house I lived in at the time. In the night, I heard some animal knock over one of the cans and scrounge through it. Thinking it was a raccoon, I yelled at it. Unfortunately, it was not a raccoon but a skunk, and my yelling startled it and it sprayed the inside of the garbage can. I didn't want to go out and deal with the smelly mess in the middle of the night, so I closed the window and tried to get to sleep. But the skunk had done his work well, and the odor was quite strong. Instead of getting dressed and dealing with the physical problem, I shifted somehow to a reality where there was no skunk-smelly garbage can outside of my window.

Of course, once I started channeling, my friends wanted me to ask Fred for information that would be useful to them. When I was doing the channeling for myself, it was fine. If it were self-delusion, no problem. (Although later, all of the predictive information I received was completely verified.) But to do readings for another person was a whole different thing.

Here is information I received when I did a channeling for a friend of mine who was preparing to undergo surgery:

Issue of communication should be incorporated into a meditative

exercise. Allow yourself to enter
the stillness of your being, and we
know you are aware how to
achieve this state. Consider each
of these issues honestly, allowing
emotions and experiences from
this lifetime, and other lifetimes
if they occur, to rise to the surface. Look at each issue. It may
be that merely in the examining
and acknowledging of the issue
that the problem can be resolved.

And, as part of this meditation,
we might suggest an exercise that
this one can perform. First we
suggest that this one, in the stillness of her heart, hold both hands
out before her at the level of the
heart, with palms upward. In the
right hand, hold a vision, or if
visualization is difficult, hold
the emotion and feeling of what it
is like to be in your current body,
with all the faults and flaws that
you perceive it to have.

Then, in the left hand, hold a
vision, or the emotion if you will,

of what you would like to be. The most perfect vision of yourself that you can conceive of. Examine these two images of self. Consider where there are similarities and where there are differences. Be brutally honest with yourself. Wallow in those deficiencies that you perceive in yourself. And when you have completely and totally exhausted the list of negative things, consider again the places where these two images are similar. Emphasize the positive. Hold yourself in an image of light and love.

Now, slowly, bring the two hands together so they are side by side, touching one another. Allow the two images to turn so they are facing one another, and slowly, have them walk toward one another, merging into one whole and shining being. Flood this image of perfection with a pure white light and fill it with all the love you can muster. Hold this light in the two cupped hands, and then

*gradually allow it to expand and
explode outward, filling the world
with love and joy.*

*Channeled Meditation
–November 19, 1986*

After doing direct channeling for about 9 months, I stopped working with this format. I found when others asked me for a reading, I would start to get information for them immediately as a flow of thoughts. I was having trouble controlling the information flow once I had activated it.

During this time, I also was learning how to use the tarot cards. Once I discovered the marvelous Voyager Tarot deck created by James Wanless and Ken Knutson, I have used it exclusively. I still channel information through my dreams, meditations, and tarot readings. I find that using the cards acts as a door. I do not open that door for another person until the cards are spread before me. Then, when the reading is over, putting the deck away helps to close the door, although there is always some seepage. The tarot helps me maintain control over the information flow, tapping into it when necessary but keeping it at a distance when it is not needed.

As I work as a hypnotherapist, I find that I do channeling during sessions as an adjunct to other tools I have learned. I find my most powerful visualizations and guided imagery work come directly from dreams that seem to have a universal message.

If you are interested in learning to channel, I certainly recommend it. The 9 months I spent doing direct channeling were like a rebirth that opened me more fully to other dimensions. In looking back through my collection of channeled teachings, I marvel again at the quality and usefulness of the information I received. I value how much my conversations with Fred helped me through a tough life transition.

If you have dreams that you are a channel, and it's not happening in waking life, maybe it is time for you to try channeling. Any metaphysical bookstore has books that can help you begin to channel, if that is your desire. Sanaya Roman and Duane Packer's *Opening to Channel* is an excellent starting place.

I remember reading Bobbie Probstein's beautiful book *Return to Center*. In the book, after having channeling experiences, she put them aside and went about her everyday life. I was outraged. How could she discard such a valuable tool? And, of course, I have done exactly the same thing. The purpose of this lifetime is for us to live our everyday lives. Experiences such as channeling and meditation are available to help us learn, grow, and understand how to go about our lives. Before enlightenment chop wood, carry water. After enlightenment chop wood, carry water.

Since I completed this chapter, I have made another major shift in accessing channeled information. In May and June, 1997, I spent a month in Australia. The entire trip was magical and wonderful things happened everywhere I went. The last week, on a 5-day camping tour of Kakadu National Park, I did tarot readings for the 9 members of the group. Being in the Australian outback under the Southern Cross and opening myself to do readings for these people was a profound experience. And, when I put the cards away, the door did not close as it had in the past. I continued to have access to information both awake and asleep. In fact, after the first set of readings, I spent the entire night in an altered state of consciousness walking through other people's lives.

The tarot readings that I have done since June have been even more powerful and accurate. In fact, the second reading put me into such a high vibrational frequency that I blew out the battery and the alternator in my 6-month old car when I put the key into the ignition.

The shift I made in Australia remains with me today. I now find it easy to access to the flow of information without needing to control it. The answers for others and for myself are simply there when I need them and when I ask for them. I am learning to live with and trust this new way of being.

8

RITES OF PASSAGE

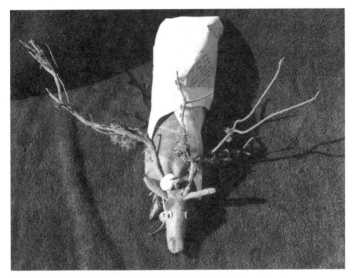

"HORNED GOD"

I am in a huge Santa Fe-style house. It has lots of levels and rooms jutting out at odd angles. I am exploring the house and I find myself on a top-level roof. There is a swimming pool there. The sun is shining and it is a

warm day. I am all alone. I
decide to go for a swim. As I
dive into the pool, the water feels
very thick and viscous. I am
swimming through this viscous
clear liquid, and decide it is time
to breathe. I start for the top of
the water but I'm in too deep. I
open my mouth and the liquid
starts to come into my mouth.
And then I realize that I'm
breathing clearly through my nose.
So I close my mouth and keep
swimming languidly and breathing
easily.

Then I notice my shadow on the
bottom of the pool. And it's not a
shadow of a human figure.
Instead, it's the shadow of a
dolphin. As I swim and watch
the shadow, it changes shape but
is always an animal form: a
whale, a lion, a bear, a cat.

As I swim and watch the
changing shapes, I decide that
perhaps the shadows can show me
the answer to my question of what

I should be doing in my life and what is next for me. I form the question in my clasped hands as I swim along. I hold my hands out in front of me, expecting that when I release them, my question will be released into the water and will cast its own shadow that will give me an answer.

As I release my question, I get the fleeting impression of a huge, ornate, old-fashioned key, and the dream takes an abrupt shift. I am now on vacation in a huge hotel room. My clothes are all tangled up and I don't know what time it is. I have a cellular phone and I am trying to call POP-CORN to find the correct time. POPCORN doesn't work. I finally call the operator and she is unable to give me the time, either. A crowd has gathered around me and is helping me untangle my clothes.

Finally the operator finds some-body, and she gives me a discourse *on the meaning of time, its instability, relativity, and fluidity. Do I want Greenwich mean time, or some other time? I say, "I just want to know the time now on the island of Maui." The people with me tell me the time, but everyone's watch has a different time. The operator says the date is January 30 and the time is 4:01 p.m. I then notice that my watch has a date on it as well as a time and it's set to April 24. I start to wind the stem backwards to get to January 30.*

The Key
–January 25, 1996

The transition I'm wondering about in the dream is how to make the career shift from an internationally-known technical writer to a healer and hypnotherapist without compromising my income and lifestyle. The answer I get is a big, ornate, old-fashioned key, and then the dream shifts to the issue of time. I believe the major issue for making this transition is likely to be timing, so in a sense the dream identifies the issue. On January 30 at 4:01 p.m., nothing earth shattering happened to help with the transition. It is not yet April 24, so it will be interesting to see if that date has any significance.

However, the really strange thing about this dream is about the nature of time. The power had gone out in my house that night just as I was going to sleep. I remember getting up in the middle of the night to go to the bathroom and the power was back on. I checked my wristwatch against the electric clock by the side of my bed. The power had been off for about 45 minutes. And here's the really strange thing. When I woke up in the morning after having this dream, the electric clock by the side of the bed had gained 18 minutes. All the rest of the clocks in the house were doing their usual blinking and fussing. I puzzled over this bizarre occurrence all day, and am still not sure how it happened. But it definitely got my attention!

The Key dream is about a rite of passage yet to come. I find that at times of major shift and change in my life, I have dreams that symbolize the shift, foreshadow the change, and show me new directions.

When I started thinking about ending my 16-year first marriage, I had a series of dreams about burials. I was in therapy at the time, dealing with the issues this particular rite of passage brought up for me, so I was keeping a dream journal. The first dream was a simple one. There was a log buried on the beach. Then I had a series of dreams about funerals, ending with one particularly rich, elaborate dream about an Egyptian burial with an ornate sarcophagus. In this dream, I was in the sarcophagus and was slapped in the face with a pile of wet leaves. A wake-up call for sure. The burial metaphor works on a couple of levels. The marriage was ready to be buried (ended), and I had buried myself in a safe, secure, boring cocoon, and it was time for me to wake up and live.

The dream in the Creativity chapter about the upside-down white ram is also definitely a rite of passage dream. It opened doors to creativity that had been blocked for years. And the ram has brothers, as shown in the following two Horned God dreams I had in April 1994, just after I had taken a weekend workshop on Freeing the Wild Woman.

I am at a workshop in a high mountain retreat, perhaps in Norway. There is much dance and movement, and I receive a wrapped gift that is a representation of the horned god. I do not unwrap the present because I think the gift has someone else's name on it. The god has antlers made from tree branches covered with moss and lichen sticking out of the top of the package. I clutch the package to my breast until I see that others are unwrapping their gifts. I start to tear the wrapping, which has depth markings on it like a topographical map of the ocean floor. A handwritten note on the wrapping asks, "How much territory can this wrapping cover? How deep can it go? Pay attention to the god within."

Horned God
– May 13, 1994

I find a bundle wrapped in burlap in the surf about the size of a large cat. I fish it out of the water, and as it comes out of the water a male buck emerges with a full rack of antlers. He stands there proudly and then runs up the beach.

Another Horned God
– May 24, 1994

When I had the first Horned God dream, I told it to a number of people. One of my friends said "You should make the horned god." An excellent suggestion. I bought some burlap and some cedar chips to stuff him with, found the perfect lichen-covered branches for the antlers, bought some wiggly eyes, and a topographical map of the coast off Half Moon Bay from the U.S. Geological Survey. I went to the beach at Pillar Point in Princeton-by-the-Sea and collected small clam shells.

I drilled holes in the shells and strung them as a necklace for the horned god.

He fought me every step of the way while I was putting him together, but when he was complete he was wonderful.

About this time, I started attending a couple of women's groups dealing with metaphysical issues. At the first meeting of one group, we were supposed to bring something that represented issues we were dealing with at the time. We put all of the objects on a table without any explanation and the women each responded with their interpretation of the objects. Then we shared with the group what our objects represented to us. It was during this meeting that I realized the horned god is a brother to the white ram, and they both represent aspects of creativity. The gift of the horned god was to create something that was uniquely mine using a new medium.

The horned god represented a new creativity emerging. In January of 1994, I separated from my second husband and by April felt that I had been sleepwalking through the first months of the year. After these Horned God dreams, I started to get out of the swamp and really begin living my life again.

Here's another example of a rite of passage or secret lore dream.

I am in a wonderful mysterious place where it is possible to learn crystal lore. It is a marvelous old house, and the room where I am has stacks and stacks of musty old tomes with arcane writing on the spines that I cannot read. To learn these things takes years of discipline and hard study, and I got in by accident. Because I am there, they are testing me and showing me things. There are huge crystals, like the ones in the Superman movie, and if you hold them at the bottom and are adept, they light up through the entire spectrum of colors appropriate to that crystal. An amethyst would glow with all the variations of purple, from darkest to lightest, rose quartz with rose, and so on. I can do this with great ease, and everyone is quite impressed with my innate abilities. So they test me with further tasks. There is a progression of crystals, each to be touched, and if they resonate properly, wonderful things can happen. The next to the last crystal breaks, and they show me how to sing it whole, which I do. It is wonderful.

Then I am in a bazaar using my new abilities to test whether things are true or false. Things that are true crystal are cold and firm, and things that are false are warm or hot. I am also finding this fantastically easy and am trying it on all sorts of different objects. Then I come to a booth were Dolly Parton is the proprietor. Everything on the counter is round and the same size as her breasts. A few of the items are false, but most of them are true, and there is one that feels absolutely right. I want it, but it costs 13 pounds 3 and 6 pence, and I have no money. Dolly said that because I am so talented, she will give it to me. So we are examining it. It opens and there is a set of crystals in it, and then it opens up and we walk into it as though it were a room. Inside are *smaller versions of the books of lore that were in the house. She says, "I can give you everything except this one small volume that has the secret key in it. That I am not allowed to give away."*

The Secret Key
–October 24, 1982

This dream is a wonderful confirmation of the gift of being able to trust your instincts and tell whether things are right for you or not. At the time, I was wrestling with the idea of making a career change. I'd been doing word processing and was dreadfully bored with the work. This dream confirmed that I have the ability to learn new things and excel at them.

When you are going through major life shifts, pay attention to your dreams. They can confirm your decisions, honor your changes, and show you new ways to move, grow, and learn.

Remember that when you are going through transitions and times of change, your dreams can be a valuable source of insight and inspiration. One of my major dream images seems to be keys, either as physical devices that are used to open locks or as ciphers that are used to decode and interpret messages. I notice that keys come up over and over again in my dreams. And I believe that dreams are important to unlocking our spiritual nature, our creative gifts, and our major life changes.

9

PSYCHIC EXPERIENCES

"LIGHTHOUSE LADY"

Steve bought two female black labrador dogs. He and I are out

in the marshes with the dogs.
Flocks of ravens are flying over,
and the dogs are leaping 10 feet
into the air and trying to snatch
the ravens from the sky. To protect themselves from the dogs, the
ravens fly behind a flock of pigeons. The dogs are not interested
in the pigeons, only in the ravens.

I am amazed at how high the dogs
can jump and how persistent they
are, but I don't want them to
catch the ravens. They knock one
raven out of the sky, and a sha-
man takes the bird and perches it
on my right shoulder trying to get
a look at it and see whether it is
hurt. The raven is very light-
weight and looks like a skeleton,
only it's black, but I can feel the
feathers, the breath, and the heart-
beat of the raven, and it is still
alive and well.

Dogs and Ravens
—June 12, 1995

I had this dream during a time when I thought I might have breast cancer (thankfully, I didn't) and was waiting for lab results. The dream seemed very "big," important, and symbolic. I told the dream to several of my friends and puzzled about its meaning. Finally, I called Steve, my ex-nephew-in-law, and told him about the dream. He said, "I wouldn't put too literal an interpretation on this dream. I don't have black labrador dogs, but I am working with a woman who does. We take the birds out to the marshes to train them to retrieve, and the birds we use to train them with are pigeons." I said, "Oh, maybe it's just a psychic dream."

This does not mean that the dream was not important and symbolic. It does mean that in my journey into the void, I extracted some information that I was not aware of concerning the activities of a favorite relative and folded it into a deeply symbolic dream.

In addition to the psychic element of the dream, I theorized that the dogs represent loyalty and ravens represent magic. Were the dogs trying to kill off the magic? One friend suggested that ravens (in fact, any black birds) represent bad news or death. However, this symbolism for the raven is hers, not mine. Another friend mentioned that ravens also represent going into the void, which I definitely was doing in dealing with a fearful topic: cancer. This meaning made a lot of sense to me. Yet another friend suggested that, although it looked like the raven was hurt or dead (the skeleton), in fact, everything was fine and that I knew at a deeper level this was true. This interpretation gave us both goose bumps, and I believe it to be accurate.

When we have psychic dreams, and I'm sure we all do, it's sometimes difficult to validation the information. In this case, I was able to call up the person in the dream. The important thing here is not the dream itself. The important thing is that in my state of mind—"Do I have cancer, how will I handle it if I do, how much support will I allow myself during this stage of uncertainty"—I opened myself up in a way that was different from my usual state of mind and perhaps incidentally, pulled in real, yet unknown facts about a person that I like a lot but had not been in recent contact with.

Here's a dream I had almost 15 years ago the purpose of which is to tune myself in to psychic emanations.

> *I am lying supine and naked on a translucent slab with a clear crystal bell suspended over my body. I am trying to receive psychic emanations from someone. When I receive the message, the bell hums or resonates as a sign of success.*
>
> *Crystal Bell*
> *–December 1, 1981*

The experience of the dream was of the circumstances and the signal indicating success, not necessarily of information received. The remembrance of this dream is that I was definitely successful in receiving the psychic emanations.

I believe that we can have psychic dreams at times of stress, both ours and others'. Everyone knows a story of someone dreaming about a loved one who is dying or who has died.

I have a friend whose father died recently. She and her mother were at his bedside when he died, but her brother was not there. At the exact moment when the father died, the brother woke up out of a sound sleep, looked at the clock, and said, "He's gone." Did the brother have a dream or did he just tune in to the energies of the departing spirit? Regardless of what actually happened, this was a true psychic communication experienced by someone who is not open to or even interested in that kind of experience.

I believe that such communications are quite common.

I am at a family reunion with my aunts and uncles, cousins, their children, and their children's children. As usual at such events, there is lots of activity and noise. I see my cousin, Diane, who has brain cancer. Her forehead bulges out. I give her a big hug, and send her love and healing energy. Then I see the tunnel of white light, and she starts toward it.

Tunnel of White Light
–January 30, 1996

In waking life, my cousin actually does have brain cancer, and the doctors thought she might live for another year or so. When I woke up from this dream, I said "Wow, I've never dreamed of the tunnel of light before. I wonder if Diane died last night." Diane lives in southern California, and the only time I see her is at family reunions like the one in my dream. Days went by, and I heard no word. Then the following week, my mother called to tell me that Diane had died. She did not know exactly when it had happened. If it was January 30, then my dream was a psychic experience of the actual event. But even if it were not on the exact date, the dream is still a psychic experience of a different nature: a precognitive dream.

I also think we can pick up random information from others that serves no useful purpose. I was staying in a hotel at Lake Tahoe one time with a man I was dating. I had a strange dream that night and I woke up with the absolute certainty that the dream belonged to someone else in the hotel.

Here is another dream that was an extraordinary experience. Was it a psychic dream? It certainly was a connection to another realm. I had this dream at a time when I was reading some of Carlos Castenada's books. In these books, he talks about going through the crack in the world as a way to get connected with the other dimensions.

I am with a group of people trying to find the crack in the world. Like Carlos Castenada, I am trying to figure things out analytically, and it is interfering. Suddenly there is a huge noise like a "whump" or a door slamming shut, and my heart starts to pound. I realize I am dreaming and think that the sound is an external one. At the same time, I am still dreaming, and LaGorda said to me, "Grab your head from behind, and hold onto the moment. Don't try to think or analyze, but just feel what is happening." A great change in mood overcame me, a sense of wonder and euphoria. I marvel at the feeling at the same time I try to discover the waking source of the noise.

Whump
–September 8, 1981

When I woke up, with my heart still pounding, I found no evidence of any external cause for the noise. Here is another dream about the crack in the world.

> *I dream about a man who is a friend of mine. Suddenly his girlfriend appears in the dream. I don't like the direction the dream is taking so I reach in and give it a twist. Then I dream that the man and I hold hands and go through the crack in the world. On the other side is a brilliant light.*

Crack in the World
–September, 1981

At this time in my life, I was really trying to connect to the psychic realms and worked very hard in my dreams to establish that kind of connection. Based on my experiences with channeling and with 10 years of psychic and intuitive work using the Voyager Tarot deck, I think the groundwork that was laid over many years enabled me to be able to get my judgmental ego self out of the way and to access information from other realms in waking life as well as in sleep.

How do you know if you've had a psychic dream? One way is to talk to the people you dream about and find out if the information matches what is happening with them in waking life.

If you dream about someone who is no longer in a physical body (someone who has died), you can evaluate how well the information or way the person is in the dream matches the person in actual life. If you dream about someone who has died and they assure you that they are fine, such a dream is less likely to be a wish-fulfilling dream than it is to be an actual communication from the departed soul, designed to reassure you that things are fine.

I have a friend who can dream psychically on demand. She can schedule an appointment to have a dream for you and to meet you in a dream. I believe this is certainly possible, although it is not something I would choose to do. For me, my dreams are such an active playground and an area for growth and personal exploration. that I would not choose to spend my valuable dream time in someone else's dreams. And, I absolutely, positively, believe that this friend can arrange such psychic appointments.

I once did a tarot reading for a woman who professed to not believe in tarot readings, although she was willing to "test me out." One card that came up for her in a key position was the Moon card. I told her (among other things) that she should pay attention to her dreams. She broke down and started to cry, saying that she had

had such strong and predictive dreams that she'd tried to shut down. As a result of denying herself sleep time for dreaming, she was becoming seriously depressed and paranoid. She was afraid that her dreams were causing the terrible events that she had dreamed about. I explained that it was more likely that her extreme psychic openness was enabling her to pick up information about the fires, killings, and tragedies that she was dreaming about. She was most likely having precognitive dreams and was not responsible for making the events happen.

It is possible to be too sensitive and pick up information about events that are disturbing. I suggested to this woman that she was harming herself in her struggles not to dream, and that she needed to deal with this information in a different way than trying, unsuccessfully, to shut it off.

Even though there are hazards in being too wide open to information and not setting boundaries, I do believe it is possible to establish boundaries and control the extent and breadth of our psychic connections in dreams. At the time I did the reading for this woman, I was somewhat at a loss as to how to help her. If I were to experience a similar situation now, I would know that hypnotherapy techniques can set boundaries that can help to understand and deal with such dreams, and even to stop them from occurring without shutting oneself off entirely from the dream state.

10

ALIEN ENCOUNTERS

"DRAMA"

I am in an alien spaceship that is circular with a glass top (kind of like a wok), and we are forced to land in the California hills. It is summer and the hills are golden and the oak trees are a dusty green. The glass lid is removed from the ship and we aliens are choking because we cannot breathe

the air. Then some adjustment is made so that we can breathe, but it makes us forget that we are aliens and the spaceship vanishes.

I am two entities within the same body and this change means that I must be split apart. The two entities are equal; it's not that I'm pregnant.

The landscape seems foreign to me, but it is at the same time strongly familiar. In the dream, I keep having dreams about this circular ship with the lid opening up in the California hills, but I do not remember that this is how I came to be on this planet.

Alien Spaceship
–July 29, 1993

Alien dreams can come in several varieties:

- You may dream that you are an alien being.

- You may dream that you are communicating with aliens in a friendly and non-threatening way.

- You may dream that you are on an alien planet with a different number of suns or moons.

- You may dream that you have been abducted by aliens.

The Alien Spaceship dream is a dream of actually being an alien. At the time of this dream, I was in a difficult second marriage and was feeling stifled. So the imagery about not being able to breathe probably had a direct correlation to this feeling of oppression in my life. I was also feeling alienated from my husband. In addition, the imagery of being two people in one body that must be split apart suggested that a split in the relationship was inevitable. Also, being split apart may have represented my conflicted self. In fact, as I write this book, I am now divorced from my husband. So this dream about being an alien seems not to be a direct memory of an experience but a metaphor for my life and for a problem I had been wrestling with for quite some time.

Many people feel they do not belong in their current circumstances or situations. For these people to dream that they have been adopted, or they are actually aliens who do not belong on the planet earth is not surprising. It's symbolic of the alienation we all feel at some time or another and these dreams may be more metaphorical than actual.

*I dream I am communicating
with the thought creatures of*

Deneb while we are watching a sunrise. The light gets brighter and brighter and just before it gets too intense to bear, I realize that there are two suns rising. The light is so intense that I sneeze, and the sneeze wakes me up.

Thought-Creatures of Deneb
–February 2, 1987

This dream is an example of communicating with aliens in a friendly and non-threatening way. Curiously enough, the bright light did make me sneeze and the sneeze woke me up. Some people have a genetic condition that makes them sneeze when they look at a bright light. I am not one of those people. However, that's the experience I had while in the dream state. I had a strong physiological reaction to the brightness and intensity of the alien light.

Silver Anglund and Pierre Anglund–I dream of alien messages, square jewels of light, a book of symbols, a subaquatic airplane full of people. Being pulled into the airplane is like going through the birth canal into

the moist humid air...and much,
much more.

Anglund
- May 11, 1991

I woke up with the names Silver Anglund and Pierre Anglund in my head. To this day, I do not know the significance of these names. This dream was visually and symbolically very rich. It felt like an important dream, but I do not remember any of the messages that were being communicated.

> *I am in an open boat on an alien*
> *planet with my father and an*
> *alien. We stop and my father*
> *says, "Now we need to get out." I*
> *strap strange tubers that resemble*
> *sweet potatoes with long crooked*
> *roots to each foot and my father*
> *reminds me of how to walk. We*
> *step out onto the yellow gelati-*
> *nous water. It is like stepping*
> *out onto cornmeal batter. The*
> *tubers keep us from sinking. It*
> *takes a little time for me to get my*
> *equilibrium and balance, but it*
> *works.*

I stand up, and up, and up. I am three meters tall. Because I never stood on this planet before, everyone, including myself, is surprised at how tall I am. The alien starts to speak in a language I am only slightly familiar with. Concepts are difficult to understand because the language is so imprecise. Then he starts speaking Deft and a great understanding comes to me. Each concept is precise and clear. I marvel at the difference a language can make in conveying certain concepts.

Strange Tubers
– May 13, 1985

In the Strange Tubers dream, it's not clear whether I am on an alien planet as myself (only very tall) or if I am, in fact, an alien as well. The key issue of this dream is, of course, the magic of communication and understanding.

Dreams about alien planets or about being an alien can be recollections of past lives. I have a good friend who wonders, quite frequently, what happened to the "other" moon. It doesn't seem right to her, somehow, that the earth has only one moon in its night sky.

And now we get into some strange and interesting stuff. I do not know whether you believe that our planet is being visited by beings from other dimensions and other planets. I feel this is so but I have never had any experiences I could conclusively say were alien encounters. I have read Whitley Streiber's book, *Communion*, and was more struck by his fear and panic at the encounters than I was with information about the aliens themselves (more about Whitley Streiber later). I have talked to other hypnotherapists who have had clients with alien abduction experiences and they say the experience is very real to the client.

While I was waiting for this chapter to formulate itself, all I had were these four little dreams about aliens: Alien Spaceship, Thought-Creatures of Deneb, Anglund, and Strange Tubers. But I wanted something more dramatic and interesting to use in this chapter. For a couple of weeks, I consistently asked in my meditations before I went to sleep for a strong alien dream or two to use in this chapter.

Shortly thereafter, I got a phone call from a young man who wanted an appointment for a tarot reading. I had a feeling he would also become a hypnotherapy client of mine. During the reading, the subject of alien abductions came up. He had recently had a psychic reading and the psychic told him that he had been "taken by the grays." This was his way of describing the little gray men with triangular faces and big eyes that seem to be exploring and experimenting with people on our planet.

After the reading was over, I mentioned that one of the students in my hypnotherapy class had experienced a past life as one of the grays, in a very ordinary situation, working as a clerk behind a counter on some other planet. We started to discuss hypnotherapy and this fellow was very excited about the possibility of doing a hypnotic age regression to help him remember his experience.

He was abducted at the age of 8 and had not been able to consciously remember the experience. However, he had frequent dreams about being taken up into the clouds and then into the spaceship from the basketball court where he was playing with friends. He also felt that, in the state between waking and sleeping, the aliens had been communicating with him and using him as a way to gather information.

We did a very successful hypnotherapy age regression and he remembered quite a lot of detail about his experience during the abduction. After the hypno-therapy session, he described the experience by saying, "It was like remembering dreams that I've always had."

For this particular person, the dreams and feelings seemed to be recollections of an actual experience. It was obvious for this individual that the memories and emotions were very real. The experience was a profound and interesting one for me. I watched him relive the experience and saw the fear, the excitement, and the confusion in his body as he was remembering events that happened to him 24 years ago.

It wasn't until a week or so later that I woke up with the realization that the universe had answered my request for alien dreams. The answer came not in my own dreams but through those of another person. Once I realized the obvious, I laughed and thanked the universe for this gift. This was yet another reminder to keep an open mind and not have too narrow an expectation for how our requests are answered. If you believe an answer has to come in a particular form, you may well overlook the actual answer when it drops right into your hands.

Which brings me to the next noteworthy event in the evolution of this chapter. A few weeks later, I went to the library looking for books to read. I was browsing the new fiction section. I usually don't look in the new nonfiction section, which is to the right of the fiction section, although occasionally something there will catch my eye. And, as I was standing there looking at the fiction titles, Whitley Streiber's new book, *Breakthrough*, fell off the nonfiction shelf into my hands.

I thought, "Well, isn't this interesting?" So I added it to my pile of books, took it home, and read it. I was pleased to see that 6 or 7 years after his first book about his abduction, Whitley has come to a better understanding of the experience and no longer feels that aliens are fearful and threatening. Instead, he sees them as beings who are here to help humanity wake up to new dimensions. The fear and panic are there only because it's scary to have our beliefs and foundations questioned and expanded. During those years, he has also received hundreds of thousands of letters from ordinary people who have been contacted by aliens and wanted to communicate with somebody who would understand what they have experienced.

In the back of the book, Whitley has several e-mail addresses. So I sent a message to WSTRIEBE @interserv. com. I introduced myself and the concept of the book and asked the following question:

I'm wondering, with your extensive correspondence and experience with communicating with people who have experienced aliens, if you have any information about whether people who were abducted and made to forget the experience tend to remember or relive the experience through their dreams. If so, do you have any information that you would be willing to have me include in this chapter, with attribution, of course?

Here is his reply:

> Often, I find that people can ask themselves to dream about their encounters, and they not only dream their memories, the visitors actually enter their dreams and begin to interact with them on that level.

Whitley Strieber
—February 11, 1996

This is powerful stuff. My hypnotherapy client with the alien abduction experience did not remember the abduction itself, but has felt, for years, that the aliens have been using him while he is sleeping. The abduction itself was not a one-time experience. Instead, it set the stage to enable the aliens to communicate with him even without being physically present.

If you have been contacted by aliens, the experience is likely to be a difficult one. You most likely have dealt with strong emotions such as fear, panic, worry, and confusion, in addition to skepticism and the disbelief of those around you. I've experienced negative reactions from intelligent people just telling them I've done an alien-abduction regression on a hypnotherapy client.

If you have alien encounter dreams, first consider the relevance of the dream to your immediate life. My Alien Spaceship dream at the beginning of this chapter gave me useful information about a situation in my daily life. Although I must confess, it is only in writing this chapter 2 1/2 years later that the information has become obvious and easy for me to interpret.

Then consider the possibility that the dream might be a past-life memory. If you're not a person who believes in past lives, this concept may be scary or difficult for you to deal with. In my hypnotherapy class, the young man who had experienced a past life as an alien found it both troubling and confusing.

And, if you dream about aliens communicating with you, it could be a very real experience. If you are one of those who has been contacted by aliens, your dreams may be an important avenue of communication. If you have not dealt with the encounter, you might want to seek professional help. Contact a therapist, a hypno–therapist, or a group of people who will not consider you a freak or an oddball. Many new-age fairs have workshops and sessions about dealing with alien encounters. Don't try to work things out on your own unless you're comfortable with the situation. Get help in dealing with your fears and feelings.

EPILOGUE

"RAM BIRTH"

I am surfing (without benefit of a surfboard). I am out in the ocean and a huge wave is coming towards me. A voice off to my left yells "Go, go, go." I am terrified of being swept away.

Swept Away
–June, 1993

I had this dream several weeks after I started a psychic apprenticeship workshop. When I woke up, I was terrified and my heart was pounding with fear. Although I felt I was ready to further explore other dimensions, a part of me—perhaps my ego—was afraid of being swept away.

And so I end this book with the Swept Away dream as a final reminder to you. Expanding your boundaries can be very threatening to your ego, which may try to sabotage you, hold you back, and keep you safely within your current borders of "normal" reality. In fact, I would be very surprised if you started opening to your higher self without any fears or apparent setbacks. I believe them to be part of the normal process of growth and expansion, a part of our aspiration to be the highest and best that we can be.

If you become fearful of change, I suggest, in your meditations, that you reassure your ego it will not be obliterated as you expand your horizons. Tell your ego it is an important part of you and you are grateful for its efforts on your behalf.

One of my favorite tarot major arcana is the Art card, number XIV. This card represents the cauldron of change in which things break apart so they can be reconstructed into a new and more harmonious pattern. Part of the process of growth is breaking out of our restricted view of reality.

A friend asked me how I knew this book was done. Her question is an excellent one, because I have been working on this book on and off for about 5 years. The process has been fascinating. I kept procrastinating on certain chapters waiting for the perfect dream to kick off the topic. When I would have a dream that seemed to belong, the chapter flowed and evolved naturally. If I had trouble with a chapter, I would put it aside until the right dream came along.

This book could well have become a lifetime's work. I have laughed as I envisioned myself at age 85 still with this book in progress and still waiting for the perfect dream. Writing this book has been an adventure for me. And as I share with you my truths, because those are the only ones I know to tell you, I realize that I have experienced profound growth and understanding during the evolution of this book. And, now is the time, as I write this epilogue on my 53rd birthday on the island of Maui, to say this book is complete.

I fully expect to continue to grow and evolve, and to further refine and expand my truths. Perhaps, if this book is well received, I will write a sequel—Going Through the Dream Door—to continue the saga and my sharing with you.

My dreams and experiences have shown you one soul's journey and evolution. As a Pisces, I dream as part of my karmic makeup, and I continue to marvel at the creativity and reminders the dreams provide. We are all part of the cosmos and are linked together in ways that are fabulous beyond belief.

I urge you to explore your own dreams in the ways I have suggested and be willing to take the chance and battle the fears to opening your own dream door. Through that door is your awakening consciousness.

Peace and love to you all.

Maui, March 7, 1996

BIBLIOGRAPHY

"Regeneration"

Andrews, Ted, *Animal-Speak, the Spiritual and Magical Powers of Creatures Great and Small*, Llewellyn Publications, 1993.

Bennett, Hal Zina, *Zuni Fetishes*, HarperSanFrancisco, 1993.

Delaney, Gayle, *Breakthrough Dreaming*, Bantam Books, 1991.

Edwards, Betty, *Drawing on the Right Side of the Brain*, Simon & Schuster, Inc., 1985.

Edwards, Betty, *Drawing on the Artist Within*, Simon & Schuster, Inc., 1986.

Garfield, Patricia, *Creative Dreaming*, Ballentine, 1974.

Goleman, Daniel, *Emotional Intelligence*, Bantam Books, 1995

Hay, Louise, *You Can Heal Your Life*, Hay House, 1987.

LaBerge, Stephen, *Lucid Dreaming*, Jeremy P. Tarcher, Inc., 1985.

Lazarus, *Healing: The Nature of Health, Parts I and II*, Concept Synergy, 1985

Sams, Jamie, and Carson, David, *Medicine Cards, The Discovery of Power Through the Ways of Animals*, Bear & Company, 1988.

Probstein, Bobbie, *Return to Center, The Flowering of Self-Trust*, DeVorss & Company, 1985.

Roman, Sanaya and Packer, Duane, *Opening to Channel, How to Connect with Your Guide*, H. J. Kramer, Inc., 1987.

Strieber, Whitley, *Breakthrough: The Next Step*, HarperCollins Publishers, 1995.